W9-BZN-690

REVISITING
THE PAINTED HOUSE

REVISITING
THE PAINTED HOUSE

MORE THAN **100** NEW DESIGNS FOR MURAL
AND TROMPE L'OEIL DECORATION

Graham Rust

BULFINCH PRESS
New York • Boston

In memory of Helen Mary "Sue" Hopton
1919–2003

Design, page 2: *Interior of a temple to Diana the Huntress.*
Figures on either side of the arch represent summer and
autumn, while below, inquisitive hounds, having abandoned
the chase, contemplate the painted landscape.

Text and illustrations copyright © 2005 by Graham Rust
Compilation copyright © 2005 by Breslich & Foss Ltd.

All rights reserved. No part of this book may be reproduced in any form or by any electronic or mechanical means, including information storage and retrieval systems, without permission in writing from the publisher, except by a reviewer who may quote brief passages in a review.

Bulfinch Press

Time Warner Book Group
1271 Avenue of the Americas, New York, NY 10020
Visit our Web site at www.bulfinchpress.com

First North American Edition: October 2005

ISBN 0-8212-6178-9

Library of Congress Control Number 2005921956

Produced by Breslich & Foss Ltd.
Designed by Lisa Tai

PRINTED IN CHINA

Contents

“On a visit to Venice at the age of twenty-three, I first witnessed Veronese's tour de force of fresco painting, the inspiration for my very first mural on returning to England.”

INTRODUCTION

Few houses can boast the magic and enchantment of the rooms painted by Paolo Veronese in the Villa Barbaro at Maser. The frescoes in this Venetian villa are as vibrant and alive today as they were when Veronese finished painting them in 1561. On a visit to Venice at the age of twenty-three, I witnessed Veronese's tour de force of fresco painting, the inspiration for my very first mural on returning to England. Forty years later my love of mural painting is undiminished.

The possibility of 'setting the scene' with a painted room is intoxicating, and myriad ideas may float into one's consciousness when contemplating a new project. However, before applying paint to wall, it is of the greatest importance to consider exactly what you wish to achieve. Thought and discussion beforehand can in the long run save a lot of wasted time and heartache.

Some of you may be familiar with my first book of mural designs, *The Painted House*, which was published in 1988. In that book I conceived an imaginary house and designed murals for every room, from the attic nursery to the basement. In this sequel I have produced alternative designs for some of the same rooms, although not all of the rooms as I decided to concentrate on those I have most frequently been asked to paint. I have also included many other new designs and ideas, as well as some of the works I have completed between then and now.

When planning this book I succumbed to the temptation to design many of the projects for my own house. As I am sure many of you will be all too aware, it is difficult to complete work for oneself when constantly working on commissions for others, so with this in mind I hoped to achieve two goals: material for this book and a few mural paintings at home in Somerton. Needless to say, I have yet to see the finished work on the walls!

The main theme that I took for the hall and staircase of my house at Somerton was based on the ancient allegories and loves of the gods. My idea was that elements of these would then manifest themselves in other rooms of the house, giving a thread of continuity throughout. This fusion of allegory and myth also includes many personal references and details from sketches that I have made on my travels.

Earlier this summer I traveled in the Levant, spending several weeks in the Bekka Valley painting at Baalbek. The inspiration I found there among the awe inspiring, ruined temples was matched later in the year by a visit to the Grand Canyon. Both places provided me with reference material that I have included in the mural designs on the following pages, and I hope that some of these may prove helpful to you.

Finally, I should add that a very dear friend of mine, Sue Hopton, commissioned one of my earliest murals, painted in grisaille. Her sense of style and great panache were an inspiration to me, and I have dedicated this book as a tribute to her memory.

CHAPTER 1

THE ENTRANCE HALL

When creating first impressions, few things can be more important to a house than the entrance hall. It makes a statement, and the very fact that you have decided to have a painted hall says something—what it is says is another matter. Whatever feeling you wish to convey, it certainly must not be dismal and depressing. Some will want it to be warm and welcoming, some may wish it to intrigue and mystify, while others will be intent on creating a sense of hauteur and grandeur. You may wish to create an element of surprise or to transform the impression gained initially by the visitor from the outside of the house. You may wish to project a feeling of calm and repose or want to excite.

Whatever your choice, it is well worth emphasizing that time spent thinking through the priorities is time well spent.

Occasionally, especially in an apartment, the entrance hall may suffer from lack of natural light. To combat this you may decide to inject a breath of fresh air and "open out" the area. It is most important to spend time alone in the space without the distraction of others. This will enable you to assess the different view points and achieve a stimulating design, effective from wherever you may be standing. I say standing because it is most probably what the majority of people will be doing in this area of the house. With this in mind, the vanishing point and eye level should be higher rather than lower.

Unless you have been given carte blanche to design in a bare unadorned space, you will need to take account of existing furniture and any strong architectural elements before you embark on a design. There is no advantage to be gained by fighting against what you have to work around, as in the end no one will be happy with the result. If those plum velvet curtains have to stay, make them work for you!

Somerton

The decision to base the designs in the entrance hall and staircase on the allegories and loves of the gods was to a degree influenced by a desire to incorporate some marble statuary and plaster casts into the scheme. It has a reasonably large window, and its verdant aspect encouraged me to use a palette of earth colours, with an emphasis toward burnt sienna for the fields of the panels. Although the ceiling is low I nevertheless opted to include it in the painted area to consolidate the feeling that the entire space was decorated. The staircase leads off from the hall, so they require unity.

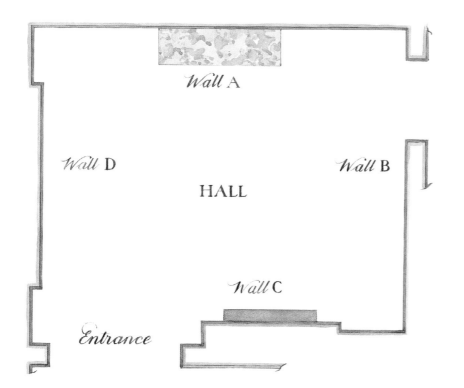

Above: *The plan shows the disposition of space and the fixed architectural pieces that had to be included within the design. A small plan such as this is always helpful when presenting a decorative scheme.*

Right: *This is the largest of the four walls to be painted and the first that you see on entering the house. Actaeon is painted in the right hand niche to match a statue of Bacchus, which stands to the left of the console table.*

Left: *My watercolour study of Actaeon represents him holding the mask of a stag. The main theme of this room is the poignant story of Artemis and Actaeon, and I chose to portray both figures in the form of statues. Here the main light source is from the left helping to reinforce the three dimensional effect. A drawing such as this is a great help when scaling up to paint on the wall.*

Right: *The main wall showing the Gothic-style console table and looking glass in the centre, with the design drawn out in red ochre ready for painting. I chose to give the impression of two niches, one with the painted figure of Actaeon, the other as a foil for the plaster statue of Bacchus. The mask above the looking glass portrays the green man in the centre of a swag of laurel.*

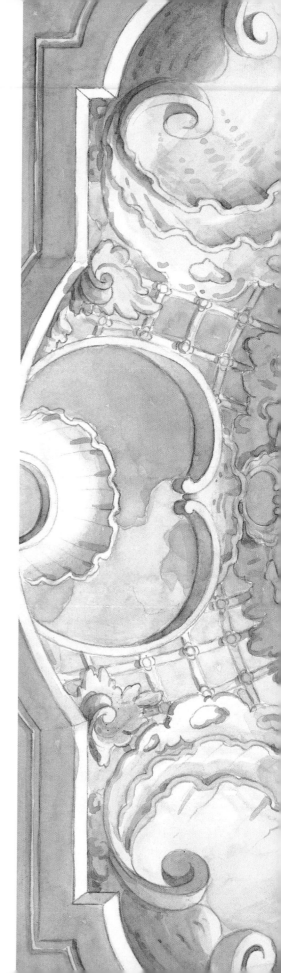

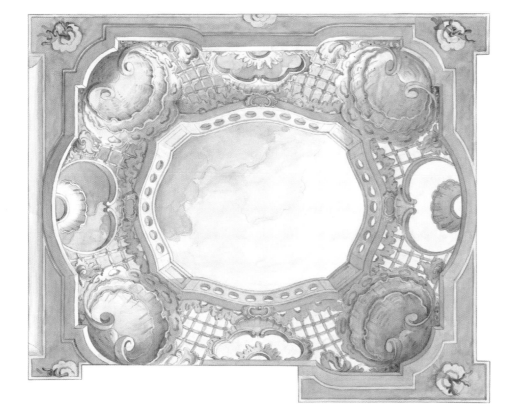

Above and right: *The design for the ceiling showing a light structure formed mainly from shells and treillage open to the sky. I have designed the substructure immediately above the cornice to take account of the irregular shape of the ceiling caused by the window and chimney breast projections. This ceiling painting gives an airy feel to the room and also helps to give an impression of height. In this instance I will wait until the painting is complete before deciding whether the central lantern needs the visual support of some flying creature.*

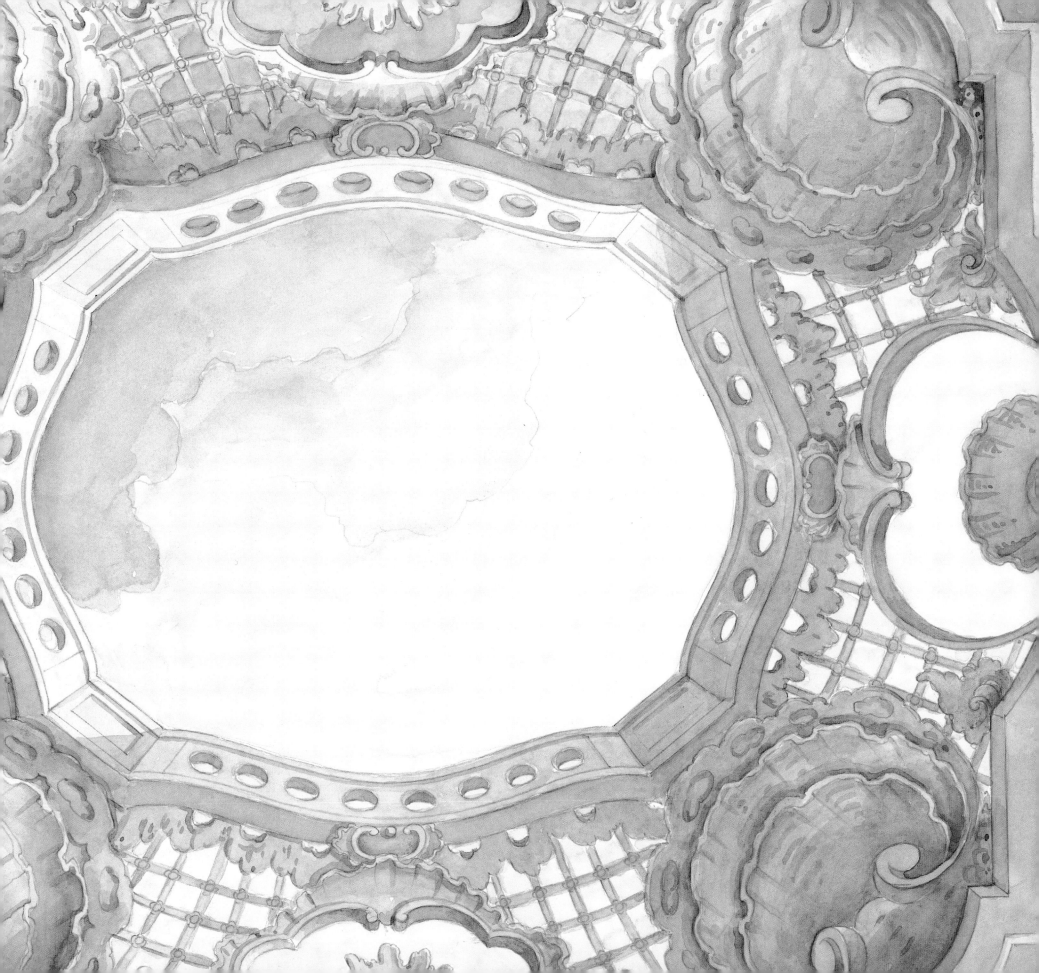

Left: *The plaster relief depicts the infant Bacchus riding a goat, being fêted by cavorting putti, while a marble relief of Hercules, resting after his labours, sits on the red marble chimney piece. The green drapery is painted to hold these together and introduce an element of colour, reflected in the looking glass opposite, to harmonize with the bosky view through the window. The chimney board shows a centaur painted in grisaille on a field of gold.*

Right: *The arch on the left leads into a passage. The arch on the right echoes this in design and gives space for the painted statue of Artemis represented by Diana with my dog, Zulu, standing in for her hound. The space between the real and painted arch allows the plaster roundel depicting two men fighting (perhaps the result of over indulgence by Bacchus) to hang above the marble lion on its plinth.*

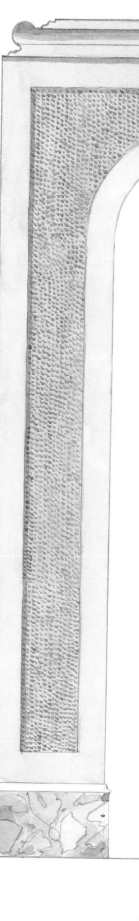

Left: *The window fills most of this wall, and I designed the panels either side to accommodate the pair of French oval plaster reliefs: two trophies of the chase. Above the reliefs there are lights in the form of shells. I decided to encompass them in a cartouche of faintly auricular design to accommodate the light and plaque. These appear again on the adjoining staircase.*

Right: *The shutters on either side of the casement. The terre vert field of the panels offsets the painted reliefs of the four elements: in clock-wise order from top left, air, earth, fire and water. The anthurium supports for the figures pick up the device used in the Napoleon III overdoor, of the adjoining staircase. Although painted on wood, these could easily be done on canvas or paper and applied later.*

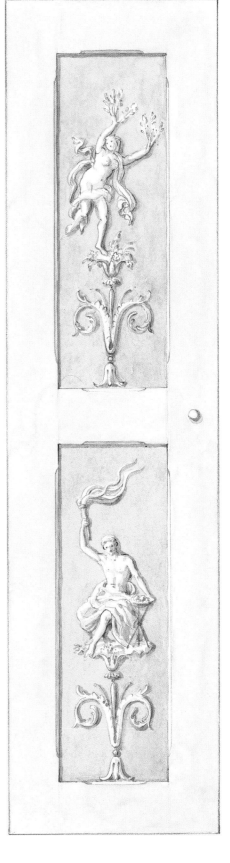

Newby Hall

Some years ago I was asked by Mrs. Robin Compton, the chatelaine of this splendid late seventeenth-century house in North Yorkshire to paint a mural in the newly created entrance hall to their private wing. As the twenty-five acres of gardens are one of the glories of Newby, Mrs Compton thought that these should in some way feature in the design. With this in mind I produced elevations reflecting the Gothic elements in the room. The walls were divided into a series of open pointed arches, to give the impression of looking out upon the surrounding landscape from a gazebo. The 'plasterwork' was painted in shades of white and the views in a monochrome of sienna and ochre. Within this framework Rui Paes painted life-sized birds perching in the foreground in polychrome.

In one of the views I have painted a large equestrian statue, which commands a prominent position in the grounds at Newby, representing King Sobieski of Poland, trampling on a Turk. The lovely gardens, as well as the magnificent interiors, mainly by Robert Adam, are seen annually by many visitors from all over the world, but in contrast to the example given by His Majesty, they receive a very warm welcome.

Left: *An owl perches on an urn in the open arch, adding a touch of colour to the otherwise monochromatic landscape. This is one of a pair of urns that symmetrically flank the entrance door. On the other one (not shown) a song-thrush heralds the dawn while her counterpart symbolizes the night.*

Right: *A splendid cock pheasant stands in front of the marble sculpture of a fawn and putto, in the central arch, facing the main window. On either side the sylvan landscape can be viewed through the two pointed arches. This design had to accommodate the radiator casing which was already in situ.*

Left: *A shell placed on the ledge in the foreground offsets the large equestrian statue in the middle distance of King Sobieski of Poland trampling on a Turk. The actual statue, made of carrara marble, dominates the view in the grounds of Newby. Subsequent to the statue's arrival in England in 1675 the figures were resculpted to represent King Charles II trampling on Oliver Cromwell.*

Right: *The newly installed, glazed, Gothic-style door was repeated in trompe l'oeil to form a pair on the south wall, disguising the jib door to a closet. This solution to a surfeit of doors is particularly suited to a painted design, as it helps to detract from the outline of the door. Mrs Compton's elegant taste and sure touch are evident throughout the house, and this entrance hall is no exception.*

Ixworth Abbey

Ixworth Abbey, like many buildings that once belonged to the Church, is now secular, having been added to over the centuries since its early beginnings.

When my client, the current owner, contacted me, he and his wife had already embarked on a programme of restoration. An inner hall on the first floor, oak panelled with one window and six doors was to be a "painted room." As his grandparents had been missionaries in China at the beginning of the last century, he suggested that I consider an oriental theme. He also wanted portraits of his wife and four children to feature in the design.

I produced designs with a Chinoiserie flavour, including a continuous landscape ranging from snowcapped mountains to a blue lagoon, to be painted above the dado level. We decided that family portraits would be incorporated in the figures of the composition.

Above: Design for the wall opposite the window, along with the adjoining wall that contains a chimney breast. The overdoor on the shorter wall needed to differ from others in the room because that door is larger, thus reducing the available space between the architrave and cornice. I opted for trellis and rockwork as an architectural device in the foreground of the mural to help give unity to the whole. I am not a great fan of landscapes that fold around corners of a room, and the use of the treillage framework around the old chimney breast helps to disguise this process. The bamboo shoots in the corner also help with the transition.

Below: One of the four scalloped-tile roof overdoors with dragons. Painted in burnt sienna, it continues the treillage element present in the design. A spot of colour and interest is added by the Black-naped Oriole and chicks.

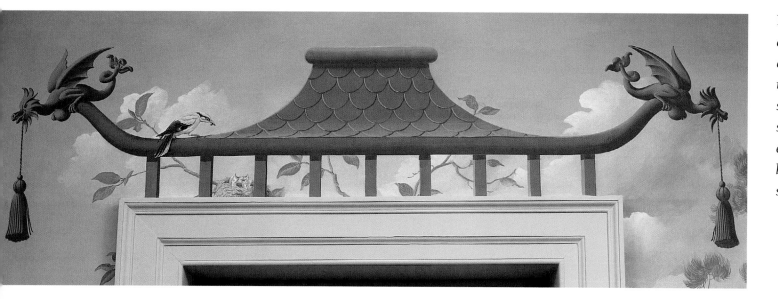

Right: This design, echoing the delicate yet mountainous landscape of Nepal, was inspired by a visit I made thirty years ago to the Indian subcontinent. The figure of a young sage, painted as a portrait of the eldest son Algie, beckons to a water buffalo, while a mandarin duck saunters by the edge of the lake.

oriental
~hele cop
pheasa~

door

Above: *The design of this wall must incorporate a window as well as a doorway. Typical of the problems that so often confront one is the recessed area to the right of the window. This step back creates a change of plane. I decided to continue the landscape, for to break it architecturally would have made the wall too "bitty." It is not ideal, but sometimes one has to compromise.*

Left: *This photograph of the finished painted wall shows more clearly the difficulty of the recessed area mentioned above. The large blue-and-white vase on its gilt rococo base helps, however, as do the two pheasants on either side of the window, to concentrate our interest in those areas and distract us from the step in the wall. Apart from the rockwork and a few leaves, only the paler colours change plane.*

Above (top): *This wall is the first you see on entering the room from the main staircase, and it is also the greatest uninterrupted space on which to paint. It was an opportunity for me to create a sense of distance as well as to open out the room. My design, woven around a complicated story featuring a pearl, takes up all four walls. When the fantasy is explained, the design will hopefully make sense to bewildered guests!*

Above (left and right): *A photograph of the completed central panel, inspired by Francois Boucher and Lars Bolander. Pearl fishers haul in their catch, two of these figures being portraits of sons Nicholas and Rupert, while their mother and sister sit under a parasol. They gaze in awe at the magnificent baroque pearl being presented by the infant in the foreground. On the left, musicians serenade the event.*

Lowndes Square

This mural is painted on the walls of the entrance hall of an apartment in Lowndes Square, Knightsbridge, in London. My clients, who had spent their honeymoon in Libya at Leptis Magna, thought that this would provide an ideal theme for the painting, and, during the grey of a London winter, be a reminder of blue skies and sunnier climes.

Like so many apartments the ceilings were not particularly high,

and the hall had several doors opening to different rooms. There was no window in this area, although the open double doorway to the drawing room let in a little natural light. There was also a dado rail in place.

Considering all these different factors, I decided that in order to give the impression of light and sunshine the irregular lengths of wall

should be painted with a running landscape. White drapery with red trim and tassels would pick up the red of the Aubusson hangings, which are visible from the drawing room. Below the dado rail would be trompe l'oeil panels of breccia gialla godoy marble.

Above: *The design for the wall opening onto the drawing room. There are no doors here, which meant that it was most important to bear in mind the colours on either sides of the divide.*

Above: *Designs for another two walls showing two different sized openings treated in the same manner, with the red and white drapery to give them unity. Adding the shell overdoors enabled the spaces in between the doors to be designed as contained squares and rectangles. The doors to the more important rooms were given a more elaborate architrave and casing.*

Corinthia VII

A few years ago I received, out of the blue, a letter postmarked Bremen. Konrad Ellerhorst, the German decorator, had been trying to get in touch with me for some time, without success. On being told by some kind soul that I was dead, he almost gave up. However, he did persevere and the letter found me, I am glad to say, in good health. It turned out that he had an exciting project he wished to discuss with me. I flew out to Bremen for our meeting to hear that the project was the interior of a large yacht that was being built in the shipyard nearby.

Herr Ellerhorst's idea, after talking it through with his client, was to have murals inspired by the mythology of the sea in various staterooms. These included the entrance saloon, dining room, stairway, lift, passageway, bathroom and bar. I returned to London and my drawing board to start designs for the various projects.

In the entrance saloon I opted for a landscape largely painted in a monochrome of indigo, the vistas to be viewed through draped calico on the three main walls. In a scheme such as this carried out on a boat with relatively low ceilings, one has to forgo the niceties of cornice and frieze and let the columns directly support the ceiling. As the client was not very keen on sailing or the high seas, it was most important that this reception area hit the right note for her when receiving her guests, wherever the boat was berthed.

Above (left): *The beautiful youth Apollo stands with his lyre on one side of the entrance to welcome you aboard ship. In the foreground two bronze dolphins wrap themselves around the columns to frame a landscape, painted in a monochrome of indigo, enclosing gentle waters that offer a tranquil mooring.*

Above (right): *The server of nectar to the gods, Hebe, stands on the opposite side of the entrance to Apollo. This pair of statues are based on the terracottas by Jonathan Valentin Sonnenscheim (1749-1828). A stormy passage may be in the offing, but here in this landscape all is peace and calm.*

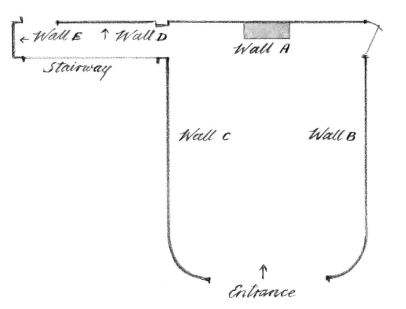

Above: *Two panels adjacent to the lift entrance, opposite the curving stairway. On the right, infant mermaids support a large shell holding a variety of fruit. On the edge of the shell a macaw perches in the sea breeze. To the left beyond the wind-torn banana leaves a palm-fringed island beckons to you on the horizon.*

Above: *This wall faces you on entering and is designed around the console table that sits in the center. To the right, a Nubian draws back the curtain to reveal a sunlit bay, while a dusky damsel proffers the horn of plenty for your delight. What more could you wish for as you set sail for the open seas.*

The Painted House

Above: *This design appeared in the cross section of the imaginary house that featured on the dust jacket of my first book of mural designs,* The Painted House.

It was the painted wall of the entrance hall. Except for the cornice, skirting, architrave and doors, this wall was completely flat. In this polychromatic design the landscape and night sky are viewed as if from a balustrade supporting urns on either side of the doorcase.

Above: *The same wall space as shown on the page opposite
but treated in this in a different manner.*

   *Here the illusion of a painted stone wall reveals a
monochromatic landscape beyond the arches containing
antique statues. This time the doors are flush, painted to
look as though the landscape continues behind the wrought
iron gates. An overdoor, of a bust in an oval niche,
surmounts the doorcase.*

CHAPTER 2

THE PASSAGEWAY

One has to bear in mind that the passageway or corridor is a transitional area connecting various rooms that may or may not be constantly visible. For continuity's sake, it may be important to carry through a colour or design from the main space connecting with the passage — a small repeated detail or patch of colour helps to give a feeling of unity. On the other hand, isolation or contrast may be your aim. Whatever your plans, an initial assessment of all the colours concerned in the adjacent rooms will not go amiss.

It can be counterproductive to spend too much time on areas that will not be seen, assuming that the majority of people will be passing through, rather than lingering. And much depends upon the situation of the passage — i.e., whether it is light or dark, wide or narrow. If the latter, it most probably means that any attempt to open it out architecturally by way of trompe l'oeil will fail due to a lack of distance between the wall and the eye of the beholder. Incorporating the ceiling in the design can have advantages

in certain situations, and covering the ceiling and walls with a design continued over the whole helps to diffuse the visible limits and give an impression of more space.

Apart from working around windows and doors, you may have to allow for pieces of furniture in your design. Lighting too can be difficult, so often one is landed with the ubiquitous downlighters, appliqués, table lamps, uplighters, or a baleful lantern, not to mention grills, ducts, and electrical sockets.

Assuming that one is going beyond a decorative paint finish or marbling, the possibilities in this area of the house are limitless. A couple ideas for a narrow passageway that might be considered are: to create a book-lined space, or to use a series of paintings in trompe l'oeil frames, such as a collection of shells, flowers, or fungi against a sympathetic ground colour. Drapery can also be used to great effect, whether in a formal arrangement or in a more feminine way, tasseled and beribboned. The creation of paneling and plasterwork also works well at close quarters.

Somerton

The ground floor passage at Somerton connects the drawing room, sitting room, and library to the staircase hall. Sections of the passageway are permanently visible from the hall and library; a fact that helped to determine the nature of my design. Other fixtures that needed to be included in the design were a pair of Gothic-style bookcases and a glazed display cupboard.

In the decorative scheme I wanted to depict a large map of the garden and grounds that surround the house, together with

representations of some of the main flora and fauna to be found there. For this purpose I divided up the wall space into various panels and cartouches within which they could be placed and then seen in part from the library.

Above: A sketch of the ground floor passage at Somerton. The two main panels depict local bird life and a map of the grounds, while mammals of the area will appear in the central nine cartouches. Sketches for the birds, map, and mammals appear on pages 42-47.

Left: *The birds depicted in this panel are all inhabitants or visitors to the garden. No doubt there are others, but not being a twitcher I have yet to set eyes on them. This composition has allowed me to group the birds together, and the small numbers painted by each one enables the viewer to identify them by using the key in the adjacent panels. I wish that I could have added a Kingfisher, our most brilliantly coloured bird, but sadly I have not caught sight of one.*

Right: *Studies of swallows after the ornithological painter Basil Ede. As it would be a formidable task to make studies of each bird from nature, it is necessary to collate reference material from other sources. This saves an enormous amount of time, and it is always a joy to peruse paintings, prints, and books in one's search for the perfect subject.*

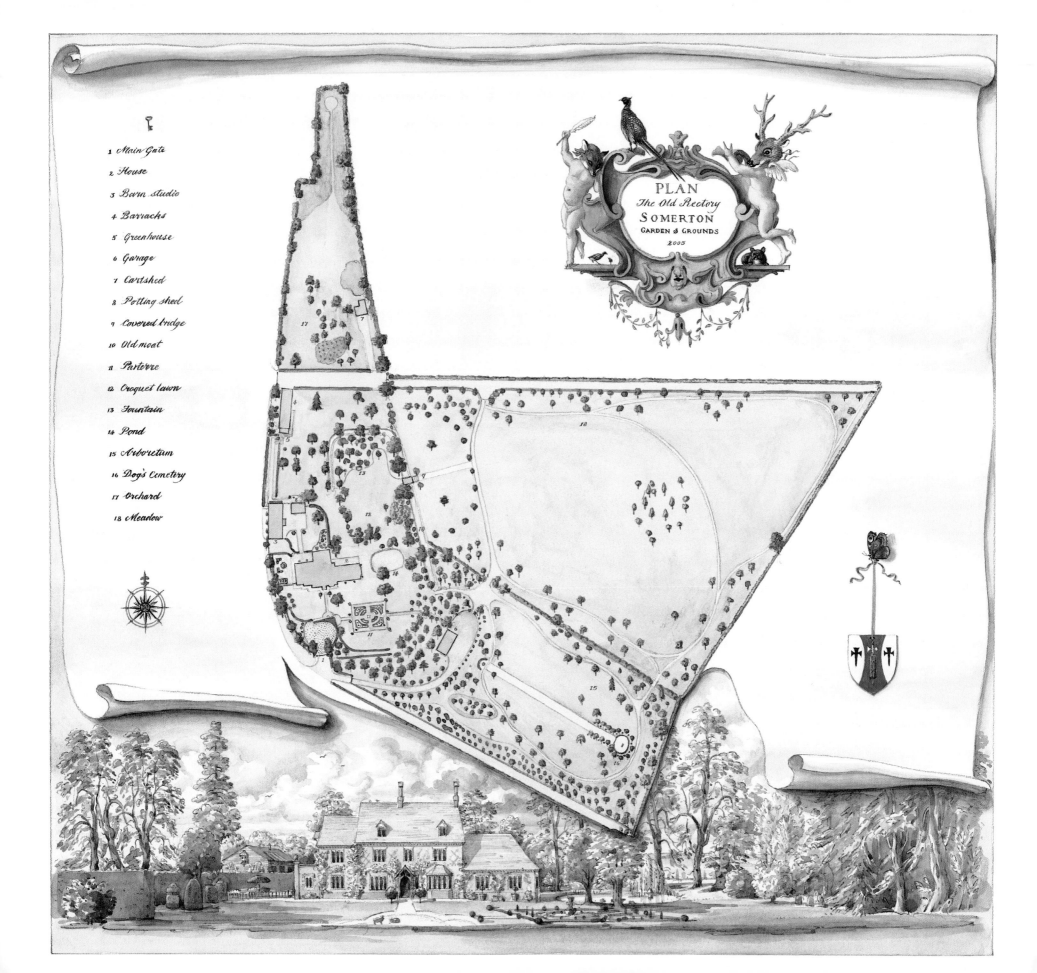

PLAN
The Old Rectory
SOMERTON
GARDEN & GROUNDS
2005

1 Main Gate
2 House
3 Barn studio
4 Barracks
5 Greenhouse
6 Garage
7 Cartshed
8 Potting shed
9 Covered bridge
10 Old moat
11 Parterre
12 Croquet lawn
13 Fountain
14 Pond
15 Arboretum
16 Dog's Cemetery
17 Orchard
18 Meadow

PLAN
The Old Rectory
SOMERTON
GARDEN & GROUNDS
2005

Left and above: *A map of the garden and grounds at Somerton with a decorative cartouche. After several abortive attempts, pacing hither and thither with a measuring tape, I finally enlisted the help of my neighbour, Peter Stevens, to produce a professional map and survey of the property. With this in hand I was then able to concentrate on interpreting it in a more decorative manner.*

To have a map of this scale (approximately six feet square) on the wall is a great help when trying to describe the lie of the land to visitors. It also enables pictorial additions to be made of future planting. The conceit that I have used here is that of the map unfurled, revealing underneath the house and garden, painted in grisaille. Two 'supporters' in the form of putti wearing masks hold the cartouche. These represent the marauders responsible for destroying fowl and flora with impunity.

Right: *Two of the nine cartouches that include the overdoor. I used this series of frames to illustrate the mammals most often seen around the grounds. Shown here are a hare and a fox. Also included are a mole and hedgehog, and on the other side of the door a rabbit sits at the top with a red squirrel, shrew, and stoat below. Each animal has its Latin name inscribed in the label at the base of the frame.*

LEPUS CAPENSIS

VULPES VULPES

Right: *The overdoor and central cartouche showing Roe deer. Diametrically opposite, above the door to the cloakroom, another cartouche in the same manner depicts a badger. All of these wildlife studies are taken from the work of one of the foremost nineteenth-century natural history artists, Archibald Thorburn. One of the advantages of using an overdoor like this is that it links the architecture with the cornice, giving importance to the doorcase.*

CAPREOLUS
CAPREOLUS

Above: *The design for the North wall of the passage. On the far left will be a glazed cupboard displaying china plates painted with botanical specimens. The painted overdoor, in the form of a depressed arch niche, will contain an arrangement of flowers to compliment a collection of botanical plates which* will appear below. Two Gothic-style bookcases flank the door to the library. On either side of these, chains of painted shells will display butterflies, moths, and other insects, and, in the cartouche above the door, a Latin legend will read, "not new, but in a new way."

Above: *The botanical overdoor, incorporating some of my flower studies. The "keystone" of the arch is, in reality, the cover of an alarm box. It was not possible for this to be removed, so I had to incorporate it within the design.*

Right: *A few snowdrops from my garden. It is a great help for reference purposes to build up a collection of plant studies. You never know when, and at what time of the year, you will need them.*

Right: *Some of the roses included in the arrangement opposite. Contrary to what many people think, painting flowers can be quite stressful as it is always a race against time to get them down on paper before they change shape. The deep red rose, Tuscany Superba, is a favourite of mine and grows outside my studio.*

Right: *Two* Amaryllis Hippeastrum *and a white parrot tulip. One of numerous studies of these plants that I have made over the years. If you are able to grow them from bulbs, it makes painting the different stages of development possible. However, as with so many flowers, they sometimes all bloom at once which can be very frustrating.*

Left: *One of a pair of roundels that I was commissioned to paint several years ago. The request was for white flowers as they were destined to hang in a particular room. By making studies of individual blooms you can then form an arrangement at leisure, using an overlay of tracing paper.*

53

Espelkamp

A couple of years ago my friend, the German decorator Konrad Ellerhorst, got in touch to ask whether Rui Paes and I would be interested in painting a series of panels for the *Neues Theater Espelkamp*. The theatre, situated between Bielefeld and Hanover, was in the process of being completely revamped and, due to the generosity of Margrit and Dietmar Harting, included an allowance for mural decoration in the foyer.

The brief was to design six panels in a manner that reflected the use of the theatre, both as playhouse and concert hall. 'To this end we decided to depict, both on and off stage, various aspects of the musicians' and thespians' performing lives.

In order to give some unity to the panels, we suggested that in each one a wall hung with a monochromatic backcloth should act as a foil for the polychrome action in the foreground. The great German composers, Handel, Bach and Brahms, are represented in the form of portrait busts on plinths garlanded with flowers, while players on stage, and in the dressing room, act out an unending drama in other panels.

Although not strictly a passageway, I have decided to include the Espelkamp theatre project in this chapter due to the multifunctional nature of the space.

Left: *The paintings, by Rui Paes, of a simian sextet. With allusions to "Die Fledermaus" and "The Thieving Magpie," they conjure up images of eighteenth-century Meissen figurines.*

These panels, designed to fit specific spaces and of varying sizes, were painted on canvas in my Suffolk studio. They were then shipped to Germany, to the theatre at Espelkamp, and installed in the foyer. There is much to be said for working at home, in peace, if construction work is taking place on site.

CHAPTER 3

THE STAIRCASE

As you ascend Balthasar Neumann's grand staircase in the hall of the Residenz at Wurzburg, you can but marvel at the ingenuity and stamina needed to produce Gian Battista Tiepolo's tour de force on the ceiling, for what works well when seen at arm's length can look very different from forty or fifty feet below. The illusion of splendour that a painted space can give is immense, and by using a design employing architectural trompe l'oeil, even the most humble stairwell may be transformed.

As I mentioned before, stamina is a prerequisite for such work, and, apart from being physically fit, patience is also a necessary virtue. Sometimes, when working on a modest scale, even greater patience is needed as members of the household try to squeeze by you

while you work. Carrying vacuum cleaners and laundry baskets, they edge their way past you, oblivious to the disruption caused. Pots topple and ladders shake, but no one knows or cares what you have had to put up with when they see the final result.

The worst conditions I ever had to endure were at the Theatre at Chipping Norton, near Oxford. I had been asked to paint murals in the foyer and on the staircase with a view to completion by a certain date. The building work was not on schedule, and as that date drew closer things literally heated up. While I wielded my brush on one side of the stair treads, be-goggled welders forged the white hot banisters into shape on the other side. I don't know which was worse—the shower of sparks, the acrid fumes, or the deafening noise. When they had done their worst, the men arrived to lay the carpet so there was no letup!

One of the most important facts to consider when designing a staircase mural is that because of the very nature of the space, the eye level is forever changing. It is unsatisfactory if the design only works from one viewpoint. Therefore, it may be necessary to "cheat" a little to deceive the eye. Uneasy perspective and sharp angles that look distorted from above or below should be avoided if possible.

Above: *The elevation of the East wall. At the foot of the stairs, by an auricula cartouche of moths around a lamp, Venus holds a golden apple in her palm. Above her, the figure of Endymion slumbers peacefully in the bosky landscape, while his flock graze by the meandering stream. Other myths are portrayed in the surrounding cartouches.*

Somerton

Following the theme of the hall, the staircase design continues with the same palette of burnt sienna, umber, and terre vert. Amorous fables from antiquity encompass you as you slowly make your way to the land of nod. The main theme revolves around the enduring love of the moon for the beautiful young shepherd Endymion, sleeping on the slopes of mount Latmos. The moon in the form of Diana peers down on the recumbent figure below, while other myths are portrayed in the six cartouches at the first floor level. They include Leda and her lover Zeus in the form of a swan, Dänae receiving Jupiter as a shower of gold, Pygmalion, King of Cyprus, Cupid, and Psyche. By the window, the lonely figure of Clytia, spurned by Apollo, sits pining as her eyes follow the sun. Shells are depicted on the faux panels below the cartouches, and echoed again in the design of the overdoor.

Right: *In this landscape, on the slopes of mount Latmos, the beautiful young shepherd Endymion slumbers, unaware that the moon has fallen in love with him. She makes him sleep everlastingly in order that she might gaze upon his beauty forever.*

Right: *The design for the West wall of the staircase at the first-floor level. In the trompe l'oeil lunette the moon in the form of Diana gazes down at the sleeping shepherd, Endymion. The oval cartouches depict (from left) Pygmalion with his ivory sculpture who became Galatea; Dänae visited by Zeus in the form of a shower of gold; and Psyche succumbing to temptation, only to lose her lover Cupid.*

Right: *I used this faintly auricular frame to "hold" the various ovals painted on the staircase. However, the cartouches either side of the window in the adjoining hall frame two "real" plaster trophies of game. The panels vary a little in size, but the cartouches can be enlarged or reduced to fill the relevant areas. The feather cresting has also been adapted in order to accommodate the wall lights above the ovals.*

These five painted plaques, together with the oval of Pygmalion on the opposite page, form the sextet of illustrations of the loves of the gods on the first floor level of the staircase. A further collection of allusions and illustrations will be painted in miniature in the chain of shells that festoon the stained glass window on the end wall. These, however, will appear as cameos in white plaster.

Right: *The elevation of the West wall on the ground floor. I have designed a painted alcove that duplicates the outline of the adjacent arch. This accommodates the radiator in its casing, and allows the painted sculpture of a satyr and nymph after Clodion, to sit on the shelf.*

To one side of the sculpture a roundel of Amaryllis Hippeastrum *awaits a frame. To the right of this trompe loeil niche, a trophy of artist's equipment and materials hangs from a peg.*

Left: *Studies of* Amaryllis Hippeastrum *that I have used in the canvas roundel on the previous page. When painting flowers, I first draw them in graphite or crayon before painting in watercolour. Sometimes I add highlights in white gouache if needed.*

Right: *The North wall of the staircase at first floor level. To the left a door leads to the passage, while an interior stained-glass window casts a diffused light onto the stairs. The shell motif occurs again on this wall, over the doors and in the chain of shells that festoons the window.*

As you look up the stairs, from the ground floor, more elaborate shell work is seen below the window. A touch of colour is added by the the bird perched at the base of the shell.

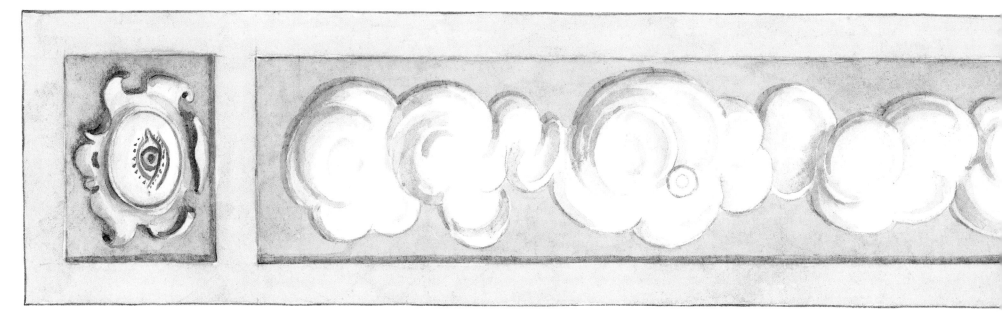

Above: *The ceiling design for the ground floor of the staircase hall. As you enter the house, the small ceiling above your head commemorates the life of a previous occupant, a man of the cloth. Dr John Maddy D.D. was chaplain to four sovereigns and dwelt here until his death in 1853. I have designed the ceiling so that four portrait reliefs of their majesties King George 111, King George 1V, King William 1V, and Queen Victoria radiate from the central dome. As yet no one has been able to find a likeness of Dr Maddy, however, should this be forthcoming it will be placed at the center of the dome, in a medallion.*

The adjoining soffit is divided into two panels, the larger painted to suggest stucco clouds floating on a terre vert field while an eye, peeping through a cartouche in the smaller panel, wards off any evil spirits that may presume to enter the house.

Park Avenue

I love New York, and lived there for four years in my youth. However, when the idea of painting a staircase over three floors was mooted, I thought twice. The potential problem was the time that I would have to be away from home. This was quickly resolved when it turned out that it would suit my friends, Tom and Jordan Saunders, better if I

painted on canvas in my studio in Suffolk. We had met a decade or so before through our mutual friend Ina Lindemann. In the late eighties I painted a mural for them in their country house in Locust Valley. That mural had been painted directly onto the plaster walls, this time they wanted the painting to be removable.

Left: *Elevations of the staircase and landing. The brief was to paint the entire staircase in a monochrome of sepia, with a chinoiserie theme running throughout, to compliment some of the eighteenth century paintings and objet in the Saunders collection. I originally proposed that a continuous landscape should cover the main curved wall of the staircase while the other walls should be paneled; in the event it was decided that the landscape would continue over the entire area, but in a simpler manner.*

Left: *The top section of the main curved wall. A large statue of Buddha, sheltered from the elements by a canopy, presides over the oriental landscape. A boat makes its way across the lagoon to the pagodas of Pai-Ma Miao, while in the foreground an old man with his birdcage sits listening to the chatter of the monkey above. This design has to work from both the upper and lower levels. To achieve this objective, I have combined the lack of a rigid perspective with free-flowing lines.*

Right: *Taken from legendary Chinese lore, the theme of this wall tells of the travels of the monkey with the white horse Pai-Ma, and their companion Pa-Chieh. In this scene a rich widow they encounter proposes that Pa-Chieh marry one of her three daughters, Truth, Love or Pity. She suggests that he be* blindfolded, *and whichever one of the three he is able to catch will become his bride. Pa-Chieh runs until he is giddy, stumbling helplessly around in the dark, but without any success.*

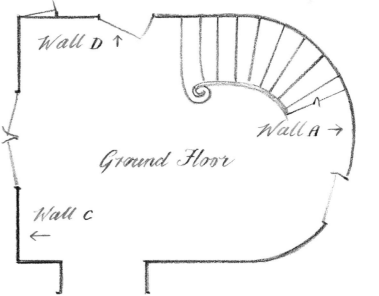

CHAPTER 4

THE DINING ROOM

The landscape on your dining room walls can transport you to the four corners of the earth, making it possible to breakfast on the banks of the Nile, or sup in Shangri-La. The Elysian Fields, deepest jungle, or desert island may all be conjured up by the artist intent on creating an exotic atmosphere in which to lunch or dine.

Nearer to home it may be that parquet to park is your objective, rolling landscape, or sylvan glade — but a stone's throw from your trompe l'oeil balustrade? I rather agree with John Constable when he said, "God save me from the gentleman's park," as a vast expanse of green grass around the room can be both monotonous and dull. Give me Petra instead, "that rose red city half as old as time," or Palmyra, birthplace of Zenobia, for rock and ruin lie far closer to my heart. In a dining room what could be better than the warmth of the earth colours on a chilly night in February?

But perhaps you have no wish to eat en plein air and would rather be in a paneled room, fashioned from coromandel or hung with trophies of the chase. Whatever your choice—a subtle understated scheme in ivory and shagreen or a bacchanal that puts Silenus to shame—it must be an improvement if the only alternative is a grim collection of family portraits.

As guests will probably be too busy finding their place at the table on entering the room, and most probably too well oiled and talkative leaving, it is likely that the painting will be viewed most often from a seated position. What is seen should work best from this level. As with all rooms, note should be taken of the natural light source. Lighting is always tricky, but as the mural will probably be candlelit at night you can count on that being kind to wall and guest alike. Should your neighbour be shy or lost for something to say, what better subject to discuss than the mural?

Ante Bellum

For this project I was asked to produce designs for the grill room of a hotel in New Orleans, Louisiana, that was in the process of being re-decorated. As is so often the case with projects far afield, it is not always possible to see the room "in the flesh" so to speak, before

working on designs. In this case, however, an ante bellum theme suggested itself for that part of the world, along with the Mardi Gras for which New Orleans is so famous.

After looking at the plans and elevations and realizing that the room was divided into several bays, I decided to have as the centrepiece of each an illustration of ante bellum life. These would be painted in grisaille in both round and oval frames to appear as if set in plaster work. Swags of flowers would be draped above the roundels,

Below: *A roundel in grisaille depicts a huntsman and hounds. Above the frame are swags of flowers, while a butterfly and other insects appear below and birds perch in the panels on either side.*

while the ovals, formed from plasterwork reeds, would have birds of the region perched on them here and there. On either side there would be panels featuring portraits of Southern worthies.

Both oval panels would be hung against formal drapery of the period, while on either side of the larger of the two, alcoves holding urns would support pyramids of cut flowers. The colour scheme of mainly blue and pink was designed to compliment the blond wood of the furniture and fittings.

Below: *A plasterwork frame of reeds entwined with wisteria and creeper supports two birds. Within the oval is a painting in grisaille of a colonnaded ante bellum house with moss-hung trees. Alcoves in the panels left and right hold urns with arrangements of flowers in pyramid shapes.*

Below: *The oval frame is painted to look as though it is of reeds formed in plasterwork, with creepers and birds of the region painted in polychrome. On each side diamond-shaped frames hold cameos of Southern worthies, while the central panel depicts a tea party in progress under a tree hanging with the ubiquitous Spanish moss.*

Below right: *One of the panels with a roundel as centerpiece, within which sits a grisaille painting showing the plantation owner overseeing work in the fields. The two flanking panels are identical to the ones on either side of the adjacent oval, except for different portrait cameos. Various insects attracted by flowers appear on the main panel.*

Right: *This panel shares the same design as that on page 76 with the narrow panels on either side sporting local birds perched among the leaves. This was, of course, inspired by the much-admired panels by Raphael in the Vatican loggia, also the inspiration for Anders Hultgren's window reveals, at the Swedish summer palace of Tullgarn, painted for Prince Frederick Adolf, c.1800.*

Mardi Gras Grill Room

This was the alternative scheme for the decoration of the grill room of the New Orleans Hotel in Louisiana. When I was twenty-one I spent a few weeks in New Orleans on my way south to Mexico. It was not during Mardi Gras, but I was nevertheless able to soak up the atmosphere of the French quarter and fill my sketch book. While researching this project, I also unearthed some fantastic designs for

carnival floats, made at the end of the nineteenth century and beginning of the twentieth.

I decided to take the parade of horse-drawn floats in the carnival as the theme for the grill room murals. They are full of joy, and I defy anyone not to be amused and uplifted when looking at them. An enormous amount of time and effort was lavished on these

extravagant creations, and it seemed only fitting to record such ephemeral works of art in this location. Each panel has one float as its centerpiece. However, in the end the owners abandoned the idea of having murals painted in the grill room.

Above left: *The float "Elegance," after the* Procession of Proteus *by B.A. Wikstrom 1904. A minor sea god, Proteus represents the bond between New Orleans and the Gulf of Mexico.*

Above right: *The float "Mercury," after Carlotta Bonnecaze's* Visions of Other Worlds, *1886. Proteus was the first carnival Krewe with a large Creole membership, and Bonnecaze was the first woman to design floats.*

Above: *Figures gather around the tableaux car of "Ceres" from* Visions of Other Worlds *by the creole artist Carlotta Bonnecaze, an elusive figure about whom very little is known.*

Above: *Proteus himself leads the cavalcade of floats in the procession, which forms the centerpiece in this, the largest of the panels. The sea god is seated in a large shell being drawn by creatures reined in by ropes of pearls as he ploughs the waves. This again is based on one of the magical watercolour designs of 1905, by Bror Anders Wikstrom, the Swedish artist who eventually settled in New Orleans.*

Somerton Library

This room benefits from excellent natural light from an octagonal skylight and stone-mullioned window. My original intention was to turn this into a dining room, to house a collection of plaster and marble reliefs, the stone floor and marble console being sympathetic to this idea. However, this came to naught when I unexpectedly inherited a library of handsome leather bound books. My own library of art and reference books is kept mainly in my studio, which did not feel the right place for these volumes. As a result I decided to abandon the plaster casts and marbles, and turn the room into a library cum dining room.

In order not to reduce the size of the room too much I designed bookcases to line some, but not all, of the walls (the room is L shaped). In order to give a feeling of both warmth and unity I felt that the walls without bookcases should be painted in trompe l'oeil to make it appear that they too were lined with books.

A marble bust of Sir Walter Scott in the window and a plaster roundel of Charles Dickens above a door helped me decide to compliment these with painted portrait reliefs of Charlotte Bronte and Virginia Wolfe, hanging in roundels in front of the painted bookcases.

Right: The elevation of the West wall showing the design for three painted bookcases set into the wall and arranged around the centrally positioned marble console table. The design of these painted bookcases follows that of the real ones, and they are used in a similar manner on three remaining walls.

Left: *The West wall showing my design, in line, drawn out by Richard Barcock. This was one of several designs that Richard transferred over many months, to various walls in the house. The next stage will be to block in the main areas of colour before starting on the chiaroscuro and slow process of bringing the painting to a finish.*

Right (above and below): *The two roundels to be painted in trompe l'oeil to look as though they are marble reliefs. The frames are three dimensional, but these too have to be painted to simulate a marble of Giallo Antico. The cameo at the top is of the writer Virginia Wolfe, after the platinum print by G.C. Beresford in 1902, while the relief of Charlotte Bronte below is based on the drawing made of her by George Richmond R.A. in 1850.*

Corinthia VII

The rain forest, perhaps one of the more exotic destinations that the Corinthia VII might sail to, was to be the inspiration for the design of this dining room onboard the yacht. However, this was to be no ordinary mural painting.

The decorator, Konrad Ellerhorst, who as previously mentioned had contacted me to work on this project, envisaged a scheme for this room redolent with nineteen thirties chic. A combination of polished steel, shagreen, and ivory was to be used above and below the dado level, and my mural design was to be carved into 3" thick panels of glass between the dado rail and cornice. I am sure that this involved some very detailed calculations on the part of the engineers building the boat as altogether the weight must have been prodigious. With some very clever lighting in the glass panels, the hostess would be able to change subtly the colour of the lights at the touch of a button.

The first step, of course, was to do some research in order to design the mural panels. After the client had given her approval to my sketches, I was then able to start drawing out the design on canvas, to be painted in a monochrome chiaroscuro for the carvers in Copenhagen to translate into glass. They produced a sample of a macaw that appears in one of these panels which looked quite stunning. The template for the carvers, a grisaille canvas, has, I am sure, found a home somewhere as it worked perfectly well in its own right.

When Rui Paes, who was working with me on this whole project, and I heard one day from Bremen the sad news that client and decorator had parted company, we realized that we too had the order of the boot. It seemed such a waste of everyone's time, effort, enthusiasm, and money, but these things happen.

Above: *The design for one of the two end walls, incorporating a stylized device at the centre, amid the lush foliage of the forest. The glass relief was to have the appearance of the work of Rene Lalique, with a variety of polished, cut and sanded surfaces. Although it would look like one piece, it was in fact to be made in three foot sections.*

Right: *The design for three small panels in between the windows. The central panel repeats the sunflower design used either side of the entrance. Above the sunflower sits a symbolic bird of paradise.*

Above (left and right): *Designs for the two walls on either side of the entrance to the dining room. A sunflower divided in two forms a link between the landscape of lush vegetation on both sides. Here and there parrots preen in the shade of the forest flora, and, according to the time of day, the sun may rise or night may fall, all at the touch of a button!*

Right: *The design for the wall facing the one shown on pages 88 and 89 using the same decorative central motif, with various palm and banana trees among the tropical plants in the foreground. They were all to be carved in bas relief, on the substantial panels of glass.*

Newfield

This country house, in the North Riding of Yorkshire, was designed by Sir Quinlan Terry in the 1970s for Mr & Mrs Michael Abrahams. The central hall, on occasions used for dining, had always been intended by the architect to be a painted room. Yorkshire has always been close to my heart, in fact my very first mural was painted at Duncombe Park, near Rievaulx, in the middle Sixties. To return there for a few months was a pleasure.

The theme of the mural was to be the introduction of the Palladian ideal to the north in the seventeenth century, with an allusion to the building of the house in the form of Hercules, resting from his labours. Within the architectural framework that I designed we included many aspects of the Abrahams life at Newfield, including portraits of the family members, their dogs, and horses.

Right and below: My preparatory sketch and a photograph of the finished painting show Hercules resting after his labours. In the landscape behind is a view of the south front of Newfield, while in the middle distance Michael Abrahams, with his dogs, looks across to the figures of his wife Amanda and daughter Emily mounted on their horses. On the right, his eldest daughter Victoria sits sketching, while her brother Rupert looks on.

Below: *My design for the wall facing Hercules, with natural light coming from the windows on the left. The crescent moon overdoor from this sketch was eventually painted on the opposite wall (see next page). Inscribed on the frieze which runs around the room a quotation from Horace reads as follows: "Immortalia ne speres, monet annus et almum quae rapit hora diem."*

Right: *The West wall showing the open doorway to the drawing room. Above the broken pediment of the chimney piece two putti lie either side of an oeil de bouf through which a third can be seen, blowing with all his might. He represents the West wind trying to move the Abrahams becalmed yacht, resting in the shelter of the Majorcan cliffs.*

In a landscape closer to home the follies at Hackforth are painted from the left of the doorcase. Birds that inhabit or visit this part of Yorkshire perch here and there while monkeys cavort and make mischief with fruit from the buffet.

Left (above and below): *My design for the staircase mural leading off the hall. On the wall of the upper flight a nymph plays pipes for a dancing faun encircled for eternity by the gilded serpent on the frame. A large urn sits in a niche opposite, while below the window a framed portrait of Michael Abrahams' mother hangs from a trompe l'oeil ring on the middle wall.*

Right (above): *An overdoor representing the sea supports a monogram in a shell surrounded by the infant Neptune and a dolphin. This sits in a trompe l'oeil arch above a double doorcase as a pair to the arch of the stairwell.*

Right (below left): *Amanda Abrahams on a grey with her daughter Emily on a chestnut gelding. The other siblings, Victoria and Rupert, consider the painting on her easel, accompanied by a disinterested whippet and, in the foreground, a curious terrier.*

Right (below centre): *A Heron sits silently by the waterside among the reeds.*

Right (below right): *Above the figure of Hercules a green woodpecker clings to the gnarled trunk of an ivy-clad tree.*

CHAPTER 5

THE DRAWING ROOM

Whether the words "drawing room" conjure up in your mind somewhere warm and comfortable in which to enjoy the company of family and guests, or a cold, melancholy reception rom that is rarely used, they nevertheless denote an area in the house in which to entertain.

The use of rooms and names to describe them are forever changing: the difference between a saloon and a drawing room—both of which might have been found in an eighteenth-century house—is not obvious. The way our ancestors lived is perhaps irrelevant, but early nineteenth-century references to "living rooms" suggest an underlying sense of comfort creeping in that persists in the drawing rooms of today—whatever name one gives them. Although some minimalist interiors are perhaps more akin to the stricter, bare arrangements of the seventeenth century, other contemporary rooms are closer to the comfortable clutter of late nineteenth-century drawing rooms.

In a grand house with large rooms, one difficulty that may arise is not having enough paintings of a suitable size to match the splendour of the architecture and plasterwork.

Here mural painting may come to the rescue. Some time ago I did some work in a newly built palace in the Middle East where the rooms were enormous. The dilemma that arose there was compounded by the fact that paintings of the human figure and animals was barred on religious grounds. That left little in the way of European paintings to choose from—even with an open cheque book, it is difficult to find paintings of seventeenth-, eighteenth-, and nineteenth-century masters that do not contain some form of animal life. All one is left with are exquisite flower pieces and still lifes from the low countries, but they do little in a room with twenty-five-foot-high ceilings.

When creating designs for public rooms, one must bear in mind that they cannot always accommodate things that one might include in a private commission. For example, a fear of birds is quite common among people, as is arachnophobia (although few of us would wish our walls covered with spiders anyway!). On the following pages I have included designs for reception rooms, from house to hotel.

Somerton

The new drawing room at Somerton was built to commemorate the millennium in the year 2000 A.D. There were several requirements to consider before the room was designed. One was that it needed to accommodate certain pictures and pieces of furniture; another was that a vaulted ceiling needed to be incorporated and then painted some time in the future.

The main theme of the painted ceiling was to be a mythological apotheosis that would include my family and friends. I envisaged much fun with the design but little with the execution. The ceiling measures approximately forty by twenty-five feet, so this work is not something to be accomplished in a couple of months. I have made a start on the designs but fear it will be a long time before the scaffold goes up. Watching Tom Smith form the ceiling from chestnut saplings like an upturned basket and then slowly applying the lime plaster mixed with ox hair was quite an eye-opener. At one end of the drawing room a large bay window looks out over a pond and across the valley, and the facing wall has two eighteenth-century carved limewood pilasters on either side of the marble chimney piece which also need to be included in the design. These, together with the looking glass that had survived a chequered history in the Turin floods, helped to determine the height of the room before the vaulting.

Recesses encase the mahogany doors that open to the study and passage. These arches reflect the shape of the opening of the mid-nineteenth-century chimney-piece, and were designed to incorporate the busts in the shell overdoor. These are painted in grisaille and represent Apollo and Iphigenia. Because the walls are taken up with paintings, there is very little in the way of mural work to do, apart from the quadratura to frame these pictures.

Right: *The west end of the drawing room showing the chimney breast that incorporates the marble chimney piece and Piedmontese pilasters. The sun god Apollo is taken from a bust sculpted by August Wredow (1804-1891), and facing him is Iphigenia, priestess of Diana, after the marble by Michael-Ange Slodtz (1705-1764). Two alternatives for chimney boards have also been designed for the fireplace and are reproduced on pages 104 and 105.*

Above: *The design in grisaille for the overdoor to the left of the chimney piece.*
The bust of Apollo is taken from the marble by August Wredow, circa 1835, and
has particular significance for me. I spent a long time on Delos, the island of his
birth, in 1976. Every day I would sit sketching among the ruins, surrounded by
a carpet of blood-red poppies that seemed to stretch for miles, alone except for
the odd boat dropping anchor, as no one, except the guardian, lived on the island.

Above: *Facing Apollo is Iphigenia, priestess to his sister Diana, after the marble by Michael-Ange Slodtz. Although eighteenth-century, this sculpture edges towards the eclecticism of the nineteenth century. The pure, smooth features are very much in sympathy with the adjacent carved heads on the pilasters, although the carving of the leaves and pomegranates is extremely robust; this is reflected in the shell behind Iphigenia.*

Above: *The design for the chimney board to sit inside the nineteenth-century breccia bianco marble chimney piece. The painting is of the infant Vulcan with his anvil, hammer, and fire. The bas-relief is in fired earth to echo the colour of the Aubusson carpet at the other end of the room. I will paint this on canvas so that it can then be applied to the board after it has been cut to shape to fit the opening of the fireplace.*

Above: *This design is an alternative for the chimney board. The fragment of stone is painted as if sitting in the void of the fireplace, rather than filling it completely as in the design opposite. The subject of this board is Apollo and Coronis after the carving by Nicholas Sebastian Adam at Bagatelle. Here Apollo is told by a crow that Coronis, although pregnant by him, has fallen in love with an Arcadian youth.*

Baalbek

In 1980 I spent three months in the Holy Land following in the footsteps of David Roberts' journey of 1839. Sadly, due to the war in Lebanon, I was not able to see Baalbek. I finally visited the Bekaa Valley a few years ago and was bowled over by the awesome beauty of the temples at Baalbek. Their scale and grandeur were breathtaking, and I resolved to come back and paint them as soon as I could. Last year I achieved that aim, returning to stay in the faded elegance of the Hotel Palmyra, greeted on arrival by the figure of Abu-Ali bent over his brazier. A familiar presence to many for over thirty years, he recently died.

Later I stayed with Souheil Haidar and his family at Ras El Ain. When I arrived in late spring, the grass was green and there were flowers among the ruins. However, as the summer wore on, they were scorched by the sun, and a hotter palette reigned. Apart from a few trips with Souheil to the sacred lake of El Yammoune, Hermel, and The Cedars, I rarely left the confines of that imperial city of the sun. Most of the time I was content to paint all day among the ruins with only a break for lunch and a nap, returning when darkness fell to the bustle of the bazaar and the twinkling lights of the tea gardens.

Left: *This design for a picture gallery is based on a scheme for the Hotel Lebrun in Paris, by Jean Arnaud Raymond. Here, the paintings in grisaille, made from my watercolours of Baalbek, are displayed in trompe l'oeil frames. To compliment the spirit of ancient Rome, a trompe l'oeil frieze appears on the coved ceiling, painted after a bacchanal by John Flaxman.*

Above: *The grand flight of steps leading to the entrance of the temple of Bacchus. I was fascinated to see the massive slipped keystone above the doorway, which had been painted by Roberts and presented to the Royal Academy of Arts in 1841 on his election as an academician. After excavation, the removal of many feet of sand had revealed a doorway twice the height of that painted by Roberts.*

Above: *From the foot of one of the massive columns of the temple of Bacchus the view encompasses the enclosure of Bahran Shah and, in the distance, the blue mosque of Immam Hussein's daughter Khaoul. It stands on the hillside a stone's throw from the largest cut stone in the world, Hajar-El-Hubla, weighing more than one thousand tons.*

Above: *Part of the walls of the Propylaea that led to the temple of Jupiter and the sacred complex of Baalbek.*

Above : *The facing wall of the part of the Propylaea drawn on the left, showing the four surviving columns of this monumental entrance.*

Above: *The great courtyard, or courtyard of sacrifices, was enclosed by an elegant portico with four semicircular exedras which would originally have housed statues in their niches. In the centre of this enormous courtyard are the remains of a sacrificial altar, and a tower flanked by two granite columns stands amidst the fallen masonry.*

Above: *Part of the complex known as the Odeon, built originally for musical performances and poetry readings. My drawing shows some of the reconstructed colonnade, with the snow-capped mountains in the distance. These drawings are mainly in crayon, on grey Ingres paper, with a sepia wash occasionally heightened with white gouache.*

Left: *A line of slender columns in this area of Bustan al-Khan at the foot of the Acropolis. In the middle distance is the blue mosque of Khaoula, daughter of Hussein.*

Left: *Facing the opposite way to the watercolour above, the rather precarious restoration of half an arch and one of the delicate, shell-shaped, semi-domed niches to the left frame the temple of Bacchus.*

Above: *The area at the foot of the Acropolis known as Bustan al-Khan where excavation, albeit slowly, is currently in progress. In the far distance the snow-capped mountains provide an ever-changing backdrop to the ruins.*

Left: *One of the graceful exedras and niches in the great courtyard. The enchanting, shell-shaped, semi-domed niches would originally have housed statues.*

Left: *An arch below the Odeon that was most probably the site of the ancient baths.*

Left: *The temple of Bacchus from the great courtyard, with the steps to the great temple of Jupiter on the right.*

Right: *A porphyry column stands to remind us of the richness of the colours and decoration of ancient times. Here the stones are a medley of purple and gold in the afternoon sun.*

Left: *Below the Acropolis a view across a field looks to the cascade at Chlifa and beyond to Pointe Noir. Only the tinkling of the goat bells disturbs the peace as the shepherd dozes under the mulberry trees.*

Left: *From deep in the excavated ruins the six massive columns of the Temple of Jupiter and the "small" Temple of Bacchus tower above one of the conduits to the ancient baths.*

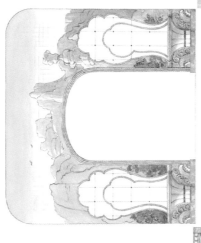

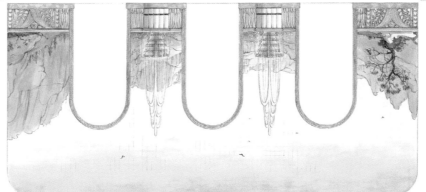

Above: *The elevations of the four walls of this double-cube room. The theme for the mural is the elements, earth, air, fire, and water, in a landscape inspired by the canyons in the south west of the United States.*

The Canyon Saloon

The design for this room sprang from an expedition that I made last summer to Arizona to see the Grand Canyon. I was joined by Victoria Adams who had fortunately arranged for us to stay with her friends Gordon and Janice Clark at Duck Creek. They gallantly drove me hundreds of miles, not only to visit the Grand Canyon but also to see Zion and Bryce canyons in Utah. These dramatic, and at times bizarre, rock formations exposing two billion years of geological past were first opened up to visitors with the advent of the motor car.

The gilded walls and ceiling of the saloon were inspired by the work and esprit of Jose Maria Sert, to reflect the feel of the Art Deco period.

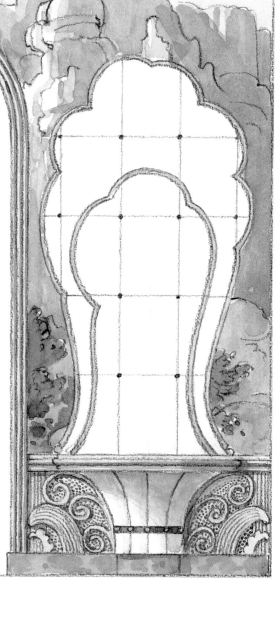

The design for the wall representing the element earth in the form of the rock mass that fills most of the area. On either side of the entrance archway there are bone and gilded bronze console tables surmounted by pier glasses.

Right: The design for the wall at the opposite end of the room which represents the element fire, in the form of the polished steel-and-gilt chimney piece supporting a trompe l'oeil brazier. This is painted against the landscape which runs around the room.

Previous page: *The design for the main wall representing the element air in the form of "balloons."* *In reality these are looking glasses, set in plaster and painted to appear as if they are tied to the "basket" console tables. In the centre, steps lead to a gazebo overlooking the spectacular scenery. Wild turkeys and other birds are included in the vista.*

Right: *The design for the wall representing the element water. Two rock crystal fountains, in the manner of René Lalique, sit between the windows, sending jets of water up into the gilded sky.*

124

The Cascade Room

This design for a Spa Hotel lounge is based on the ambient waters of Pamukkale.

When travelling in Turkey in 1990, I climbed the steep cliffs above the plain of Curuksu to paint the calcified terraces of Pamukkale and the thermal waters made popular in the Imperial period that flourished in the second and third centuries A.D. Some time ago I stumbled upon these watercolours while trying to sort out the chaotic portfolios of drawings in my studio. This sparked the idea for a mural based on the myth of Leda and the swan—in particular, the W.B. Yeats couplet, "Love and war came from the eggs of Leda." I have, over the years, harboured a desire to use in a wall painting, a fantastic arrangement of barnacles on a giant scale, and I hoped to combine the two ideas. I have always collected shells, corals, and crustaceans on my travels, and one of my favourites to paint is the barnacle, coming

Left: *One of the arches on either end of the room. The walls and ceiling are silvered— i.e., Dutch metal with lacquer. The room is a double cube with skylights, and measures forty by twenty feet.*

as it does in so many shapes and sizes. In the design these barnacles give a structure to the room. On the main wall a cascade of water flows down from a source above and is then purified by crustacea before flowing through subterranean ducts and breaking out into the open valley depicted on the facing wall.

Leda, a symbol of fertility and renewal, is surrounded by her offspring, while everything around her is bursting into life. For those visiting the spa this would represent the act of cleansing and hopefully provide an oasis of cool and refreshment during the long hot summers.

Below: *The window wall with Leda and the signets in the purified waters of the river of life that becomes the Meander. At night the arched casements of the windows hold mirrored-glass sliding shutters that reflect the light of the chandeliers on the silvered walls.*

Right: *The main wall of the lounge with its silvered sky, barnacles, and cascade. It could be overwhelming if it were not for the open arches on either side and the distant landscape opposite. I suggested the floor be made of marble from Turkish quarries, with a border and inserts of violet aezani to the main field of ice blue proconnesos. This would be offset by the white linen covers of the ottoman and chairs.*

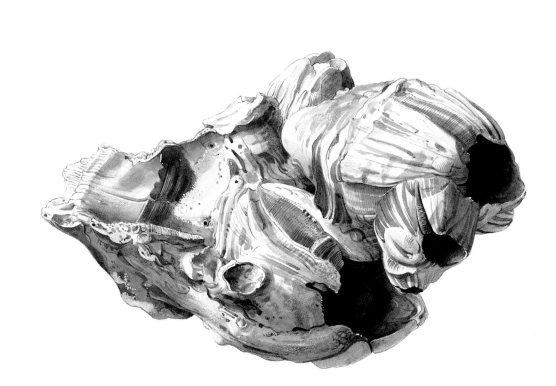

Above: *A watercolour study of a piece of barnacle that I came across in the south of France. The delicate pinks, violets, and greys are a joy to paint. It is always helpful to make a drawing from nature as the structure is then more easily understood, enabling you to adapt and create other forms more easily.*

Right: *One of the end walls with its adjacent walls, showing how one might adapt the barnacle form to "turn" the corners where they meet.*

Al Bustan

The Al Bustan hotel at Beit Meri overlooking Beirut, has much to offer apart from refuge from the hustle and bustle of the city. Music lovers stay every year for the music festival, while other guests and travellers enjoy the choice of cuisine offered by the various restaurants in the hotel. For those interested in antiquity the Maronite monastery of Deir Mar Yuhanna Qalaa nearby occupies a small area of the Cella of the temple to Baal Marquod, built on the site of an earlier Phoenician temple.

Most of the ancient sites and places of ineterst in this small country are within a day's drive. It was while I was painting a mural in Manara, in Beirut, that I went up to the al Bustan, at the request of my friend and client Myrna Bustani, to measure up for some mural panels for the hotel. Four "Presidential" suites were being done up, and all four were identical in layout, having a sofa in the recess of each sitting room. The idea was to open up the rooms with vistas of calming sylvan landscapes on the walls behind the sofas. In every case the colours in the rooms had to be reflected in the paintings.

Left: *My watercolour study of a miniature rose in a cachepot. This was painted to be used in the foreground of one of the panels to help give a feeling of distance to the landscape behind.*

Left: *A pink made from burnt sienna was used for the drapery, to pick up the hues of the upholstery in the sitting room. The terracotta pots also help to reflect a darker shade in the palette of earth colours. The panels were painted on canvas in my studio and then shipped out and applied to the walls in situ.*

Left: *In this panel an arch forms part of the framework with drapery above. The rose in a cachepot on the opposite page sits on a ledge in the foreground. The vista of a watery sylvan landscape with a temple will hopefully be soothing to the guests facing it.*

CHAPTER 6

THE BEDROOM

For somewhere that the majority of us will spend a third of our lives, the decoration of the bedroom needs careful consideration. Whether your preference is for a polonaise bed or a simple divan, the ambience needs to be conducive to rest and repose as you slip into the world of dreams. For many their bedroom is the only truly private space in the house, a sanctuary, not to be violated by the taste of others. Before putting pen to paper it is best to determine the overall colour scheme and then the subject matter of the painting. If a guest room, do remember that what might entrance your great aunt may not be appreciated by your trigger-happy godson.

The mural painter should try to be prepared for most things when arriving to work in someone else's house, and he or she needs to take the owners' foibles and fancies in his stride. However, some time ago I was commissioned to paint an over mantel in the bedroom of the house of an American woman living in London, and I was in for a surprise. Arriving on my first day

at a civilised hour, the pre-arranged time of ten a.m., I was shown upstairs to her bedroom by the housekeeper who opened the door for me and departed. A large four-poster bed dominated the room. The bed appeared to be unmade, but I only realised that I was not alone when the mound of bedclothes suddenly moved. A bleary eyed tousled head appeared for half a second only to retreat beneath the sheets. I continued setting up my table and started to square up my design only to be jolted out of my reverie by a yawn. As I turned around a young man in silk pyjamas climbed out of the bed, then, with a brief nod, disappeared, presumably to bathe and dress.

He turned out to be the laconic lover of my client, a tennis pro of a lazy disposition! The pattern continued all week long—he never surfaced much before noon. When I had finished, the immaculately made up American lady sidestepped the subject with great aplomb and bade me farewell without any reference to her indolent paramour.

The Pink Bedroom

Pink in colour and pink in subject, this bedroom is an alternative to the blue-and-white room that appears in the cross section of the imaginary villa reproduced on the dust jacket of *The Painted House*.

Here I have divided up the walls of the rooms with a series of trompe l'oeil panels, above and below the dado rail. The rococo decoration inside the panels reflects the spirit of the eighteenth-century terra cotta relief of Flora in the panel above the fire-place. Surrounding Flora is a garland of lilies and roses together with other flowers.

In each of the panels a variety of dianthus is depicted. The panels continue around the room in the same manner on either side of the doors and window. Facing the fireplace, a canopied sofa bed more or less obscures the main central panel. Below the dado rail, panels of shells are painted in monochrome. In principle the designs for this room could very easily be adapted to one of a different size by increasing or decreasing the number of panels.

The chimney board that I designed for the fireplace is shown in the small design on the preceding page, a portrait of my beloved French bulldog Bella. However, should the bedroom be commissioned by a client, her feline friend or precious pooch could star instead.

Right: The fireplace wall with the central panel showing a terra cotta plaque of Flora after Clodion, surrounded by a garland of flowers. Within the other four panels specimens of pinks take pride of place. As an alternative to marble, the breche violette on the bolection moulding could be painted on wood.

Left: *The canopied sofa bed dominates this wall, almost obscuring the central panel. In this situation where a bed or piece of furniture makes a painted panel redundant, only the simplest decoration need be included to complete the scheme.*

Below: *One of the burnt sienna monochrome paintings that feature in the design for the panels below the dado rail. Each shell in the room is different and has coral, seaweed, or aquatic flora included in the arrangement.*

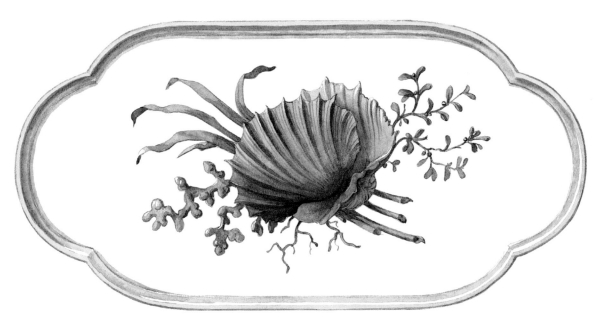

Below: *This beautiful rose, "Souvenier de la Malmaison," was painted at the behest of one of my youngest clients, Georgina Ellis. The rose, which grows against the walls of my studio, is very susceptible to damp which makes its blooms all the more precious.*

Left and above: *A garland of roses and pinks, tied with a ribbon, encircles a gilded letter "S" inset with pearls. This was a design for my friend, Sue Hopton, in memoriam, and I have used it here to demonstrate how such a painting could be incorporated in a scheme for a chimney-board.*

The design is of the simplest nature, showing how flowers can be arranged around an initial. Here the garland and initial are the central image in the recessed panel of the marble bolection moulding that surrounds the fireplace.

Above and right: *These old roses grow in a sunny, sheltered position near my studio, which is a great help when I need a specimen to paint. I endeavour to make as many studies as possible when they bloom as inevitably when one needs one they are not in flower. Variegated roses are a particular favourite of mine; this one is Veriagata de Bologna, Lodi 1909.*

Above: *While making studies of various plants for a new edition of*
Some Flowers *by Vita Sackville-West, I too was captivated by the*
"cheddar pink" of which she writes so eloquently. These double pinks
are not from the laureate's garden but my own, picked on a summer's
evening to paint the following day.

Below: *The charm of this lovely, fragrant, bourbon rose, Souvenier del la Malmaison, Beluze 1843, with its pale cream blush pink, is hard to beat. These three studies were made for the painting on page 141. I usually make separate drawings of flower and leaf, as time is of the essence with these blooms. Leaves and flowers are then combined at a later date, when the pressure is off.*

The Chinese Room

The land of Cathay has inspired artists and craftsmen ever since the first intrepid travellers in the middle ages returned to Europe to regale those at home with tales of the fabulous treasures of the Orient.

Chinoiserie reached a high point in the late seventeenth century, and in the eighteenth century with the flowering of the Rococo style, this affected almost every area of the decorative arts. Even when neo-classicism and the Gothic revival held sway, the flame was never extinguished, and it still holds great fascination today.

Some time after the Berlin wall came down, I visited Potsdam, and will never forget coming upon the Chinese Tea House at Sans Souci. By a gilded column shimmering in the late afternoon sun, the solitary figure of a Chinese youth stood playing the violin. As we wandered by, the poignant strains of Tchaikovsky followed us, floating through the trees.

Nearer to home, the work of the wood carver Luke Lightfoot at Claydon House in Buckinghamshire, is a feast for the eyes. This delicious fantasy was created for Lord Verney in the 1760s. The design for this painted bedroom is a far simpler evocation of the Chinoiserie spirit, being a series of trompe l'oeil plasterworks, on fields of blue, in panels. The room was commissioned by an expert gardener, who was quite happy to wake at dawn to see trophies of gardening implements as gentle reminders of her day ahead.

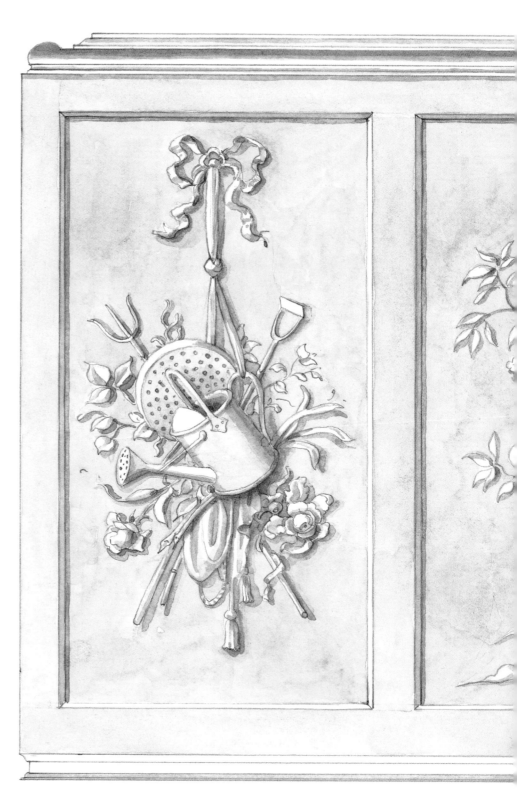

Right: *One of the two main walls of the bedroom showing an exotic tree in the centre panel, flanked by two trophies of gardening implements on either side.*

Right: *The design for the central panel shows a Chinoiserie-inspired gateway, flanked by panels with flowering trees. In order to create movement in the blue field of the panels I have given the initial wash of colour an overlay of dots of the same hue. You can see the difference this creates in the half-finished background of the watercolour.*

Upper Belgrave Street

I should have known that monkeys in Belgravia were not the order of the day. Cultural sensibilities are just one of the constraints that have to be considered when embarking on a design. I had worked previously for this Middle Eastern client but, nevertheless, I should have heeded my own dictum and discussed the project more thoroughly beforehand. After talking it through, the decision was made to paint song birds instead of the monkeys, thereby replacing one element of life and colour with another, in the essentially

monochromatic scheme. The result, I am glad to say, was a success.

This room was just one of many in the house that was undergoing major refurbishment, and working there turned out to be a watershed in my life. Different crews of painters, joiners, decorators, and electricians all jostled for position, under the watchful eyes of security men, trying not to trip over, dislodge, or hinder each other's work. Wrung out at the end of the day with nowhere to wash or change, Rui Paes and I, dusty and dishevelled, would walk around the corner to

Eaton Place, past my old flat at number 30, scene of happier times, and make our way down the street to Chelsea, where the car was parked in a residents' bay. I resolved then and there never to work on site in London again!

Below left and right: The two main walls of the room showing the monkeys on the left and the birds on the right. The other walls were taken up mainly by mirror glass, chimney piece, and doors.

Corinthia VII

This design is included here because today it seems to be the norm that bedroom and bathroom are ensuite, particularly in any contemporary construction such as this yacht. Long gone are the days of only one bathroom for a large house, although I well remember, in the middle sixties, staying with Lady Meade-Fetherstonhaugh at Uppark, and being woken in the morning by footmen bringing a brass can of hot water with which to shave.

It is the improvements in plumbing that so often have left us with rather cut up and awkward spaces in bathrooms. Due to the number of ducts, vents, pipes, electrical wiring, and other necessities, even a

brand new room may have little space left uninterrupted on which to paint. It is no use ignoring these facts—one bête noir of mine is to see mural painting continued over radiator, pipe, cornice, and skirting board. Far better, if need be, to paint out the radiator in a colour or tone that harmonizes with the whole.

Being on a yacht, this bedroom had relatively low ceilings which meant that the area to paint above the dado was limited and very much cut up by doors, cupboards, looking glass, and window. I decided to incorporate these by creating various panels in a faintly Chinoiserie manner, some to contain landscapes, some niches to hold

flowers, and others to be of trellis. If they had all been landscapes, I think it would have been a little too busy and claustrophobic. The trellis not only gives the eye some relief, but also solves the problem of how to treat the very narrow panels.

The landscapes are of a series of temples and kiosks painted in sepia, and the niches contain pots of flowers to give accents of colour and softness to the room. A bathroom adjoins the bedroom, possibly with a door open much of the time, so the two must interact harmoniously, whatever the colour scheme may be.

Above: The elevation of the bathroom walls showing the combination of different panels—i.e., landscape, trellis, and niche with flowers. As you see, the panels vary in size, with the trellis very much adapted to fit the space between the more elaborate panels.

Above and below: *This window wall illustrates perfectly the difficulties involved when not painting in situ. So many odd shapes, bits, and pieces painted on canvas in the studio, need to be well documented and hung by an expert paper hanger. Measurements need to be double checked, as nothing can be more disappointing or annoying than to find the finished work too big or too small.*

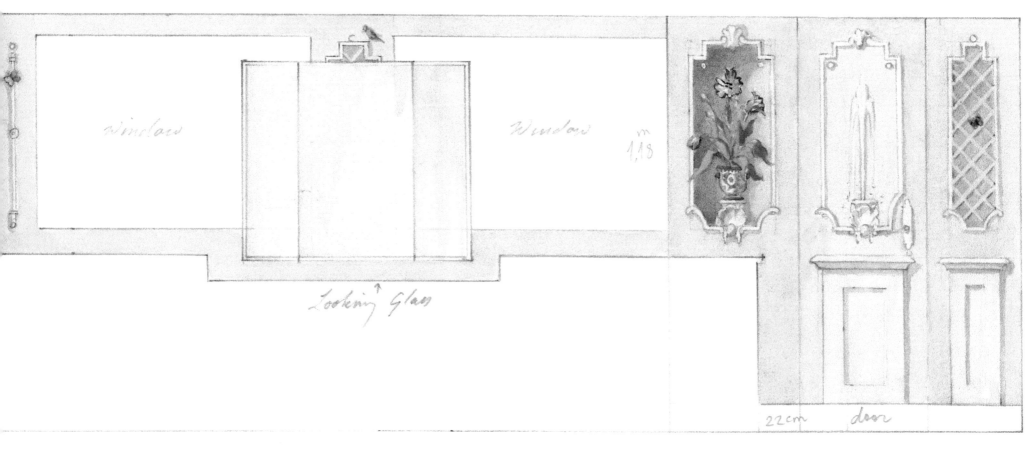

Above: *Two watercolour studies of auriculas with their rich, velvety corollas and stiff, curly leaves. The task of painting these is a relief after anxious hours spent on a rose, praying that it will not open any more and change shape completely. The auricula makes a good subject for anyone new to flower painting.*

Right: *The parrot tulip, Estelle*
Rheingold. I painted this as a pair to
the black parrot tulip opposite for an
exhibition that I held at Marlborough
House in 1999, in aid of Sight Savers.
The original watercolours were then
used to make silk-screen prints in a
limited edition of 250 each.

Left: *The black parrot tulip in its Delft cache pot. The studies that I made of this delicate but faintly sinister bloom are invaluable when it comes to composing flower pieces (as in the case of the niches in the bathroom design). It is necessary to paint them from varying angles to make a satisfactory composition.*

157

Left and below: *An amaryllis and two studies of the same tulip. The amaryllis signifies splendour in Greek, and this dazzling specimen certainly lives up to its name with white petals brushed with scarlet, like the powdered face of the geisha.*

Above: As with many things in life, it is not always the perfect specimen that is the most desirable. In the case of flora, a tormented, twisted leaf or spotted petal can give a curious interest to an otherwise straightforward rendering of the plant.

159

CHAPTER 7

PANELS AND PRACTICE

In this book I have attempted to show designs for the areas of the house most often requested for mural painting. On the following few pages I have included some projects and panels that do not fall neatly into the preceding chapters—i.e., designs for a theatre vestibule, a memorial panel in a chapel, two swimming pool houses, and an overdoor. I have also included some information on my working methods.

Some of the designs in the book inevitably overlap and can be interchanged from room to room, but there are also areas of these designs that can easily be extracted and used elsewhere on a smaller scale. One example of this is the design for the library at Somerton, where I have extracted a section to be used in the

sitting room. I decided to alter a fitted bookcase in this room by having open frame doors, with chicken-wire panels, made for the three sections. The middle one is now a cupboard with a trompe l'oeil collection of books painted on a panel that sits behind the wire. At a casual glance, all three sections look as though they are filled with books, both real and painted, whereas the reality is that the middle one now holds boxes of papers and oddments, all neatly out of sight. The whole panel measures approximately 60" x 18" with the painted canvas marouflaged to the board. It could, of course, be painted directly onto the primed board, and the trompe l'oeil books could equally be replaced by china or objet d'art on the shelves.

Working on a small panel is a good way to start for those new to mural painting. However, it is important not to be lulled into overworking the painting. Standing on a ladder or kneeling on the floor encourages one to get down to the essentials as it is too uncomfortable to be fiddle-faddling about for too long.

It is difficult to know what instruction will be helpful and what is obvious as some readers will be novices, others old hands. However, books on paint techniques abound for those who wish to pursue further research. Here I have concentrated mainly on the way that I work, and the paints and materials that I use when painting murals.

Above: *Designs for two walls. On the first, the Two Ugly Sisters accompanied by Puss-In-Boots sit in the box; below them, on either side of the window, hang a scroll and Red Riding Hood's cape.*

On the adjoining wall, Widow Twanky clutches one end of a sheet depicting the torsos and legs of dwarves dancing on a tightrope. The heads of the actors are visible above the sheet. To the right is Prince Charming with Cinderella.

The Theatre, Chipping Norton

The theatre at Chipping Norton, formed twenty-five years ago from a Salvation Army citadel and a few cottages, underwent a face lift when the National Lottery Fund made a grant to extend the stage and redo the interior. An allowance had been earmarked for mural decoration, and Tamara Malcolm, the founder and moving force behind the theatre, approached me to discuss the project. Although numerous performances are staged throughout the year, including plays, music, dance, and film, the theatre is best known for its pantomime season and this was the proposed theme for the mural.

The area to be painted was an unusual shape extending over two floors conjoined by a circular staircase and balustraded walkway at the upper level. The design at this level included actors in a performance viewed through a proscenium arch on one wall, while characters from pantomime, sitting in boxes on the adjacent and facing walls look on. The archways on the staircase open up to a starlit view of Chipping Norton with a statue of Dick Whittington in the foreground. My godson, Hugh Bickerton, kindly posed for this figure as well as for Harlequin and Prince Charming, while friends Mary Sheepshanks and Henrietta Pope posed for others.

On the ground floor portraits of thespians and other theatrical references are painted around the wall of the bar to amuse the punters while they enjoy a drink during the interval.

Left: The watercolour study for the oil painting. A silk screen print of this study was made in a limited, signed edition of 200 copies to fund the memorial.

Father Napier Memorial, St Wilfrid's Chapel

I was asked by Prince Rupert Loewenstein to design a panel to hang in St. Wilfrid's Chapel at the Brompton Oratory as a memorial to his friend, Father Michael Napier. Father Napier, who was elected provost of the London Oratory five times, collapsed in 1996 at St Wilfrid's altar, close to the tomb of the first superior of the London Oratory, Father Wilfrid Faber. He died soon after.

Prince Rupert's suggestion was to represent the founder of the Oratorium, St. Philip Neri in Rome, and Father Napier, centuries later, carrying the torch in London. To this end, my design included bronze busts on plinths of both men against a background of their respective cities. Between the two, an urn signifies the Holy Trinity while Our Lady is represented by a lily in the central niche. A gold finch, symbol of The Passion of Christ, alights by the holy water. Above this niche, angels support the Napier coat of arms.

Right: Drapery always looks unconvincing if it is painted from the imagination; time spent on making a study from cloth of the right hue and tone will, in the end, save time.

165

Dartmoor

In the mind, Dartmoor and the scene to the right seem miles apart, which was the object of the exercise. I was asked to design a landscape to be painted on the end wall of a swimming pool house, near Chagford on the edge of Dartmoor. The owner wanted to create an atmosphere of summer climes for the short dark days of winter. Taking the natural arch on the coast of Posillipo for my inspiration, I proposed that the illusion beyond the pool should incorporate a blue lagoon in a tropical landscape with monkeys picnicking among the flora and fauna in the foreground.

However, the client's wife did not like monkeys, so they were dispatched in the final painting and replaced with the arch enemy of the song birds on page 150, cats. I painted the canvas in my studio, and then it was installed with great difficulty on the curved wall at the end off the pool, temperature and humidity always being a problem in these situations.

Left: *In my early twenties I stayed at Tabley in Cheshire, the splendid red sandstone house by Carr of York, while painting a portrait of the owner, Colonel Leicester Warren. It was winter, freezing cold, and my bedroom was enormous. There was no heating apart from the smallest single-bar electric fire I have ever seen—-about 6" wide, a relic of the nineteen twenties. However, among the paintings hanging on the wall was the most beautiful watercolour of a pineapple by J.M.W. Turner. I fell in love with it, and it remains frozen in my memory! Many years later I painted the one reproduced here.*

Right: *The initial watercolour design for the swimming pool house, showing the monkeys under the awning; these were later replaced by cats.*

Above (top): *The design for the central wall showing a thieving monkey making off with a necklace, while on the lake some ducks swim gently by.*

Above: *A mandarin duck dominates the right hand wall. The patterns and varied shapes of the leaves and foliage help to give interest and movement as well as introducing a lush atmosphere around the pool.*

The Vale

This frieze was designed for a swimming pool that was constructed in the garden of a Chelsea house in London.

Above the four-foot frieze which sits at ground level, there is a pitched roof of glass which floods the pool with light in the daytime. The frieze is formed of fixed panels running around three sides of the pool, and had to be painted in situ. Rui Paes, who painted the birds and monkey, and I spent a rather arduous few weeks kneeling or crouching on the floor to paint the mural, but that concentrates one's mind on the essentials!

Including the water fowl and lake in the landscape helped to extend the aquatic atmosphere and soften the surrounding 20' x 20' area. The monkey was added to amuse the children, and is depicted making off with a piece of jewelry, while the owner is in the pool. An incident not dissimilar to this happened to me when painting some temples in Nepal. A monkey snatched my camera, and ran away with it along a parapet and then up into the trees, never to be seen again. Whether this was orchestrated by the local Fagin, or just the monkey having some fun I don't know, but as a consequence I am much more careful with my impedimenta when sketching in similar situations.

Above: *The design for the left hand side wall with two Canada Geese as the focal point. They stand full size in the foreground which helps to push the landscape back. The far distance is always painted first, gradually working forwards. The birds are then painted and the tone and colour adjusted to the background. There is a certain amount of to-ing and fro-ing as sometimes you may wish to strengthen or weaken an area of the painting.*

Above: The design shows the paneled cupboard doors on either side of the recess, holding a marble bath with a looking glass above it. The plates are painted in a symmetrical arrangement within the panels, and the colours in the botanical painting are used elsewhere in the room's decoration. This is an example of a room being decorated around a painting and thus not having to work within a pre-existing colour scheme.

Le Mubry

The trompe l'oeil paintings in this bathroom were inspired by a collection of Chelsea Red Anchor porcelain belonging to a friend. Her grandparents had created the collection over the years by adding to it on each wedding anniversary with their exchange of gifts. Every piece has botanical decoration or is made in the form of a fruit or vegetable tureen.

Here I have chosen to arrange plates and dishes within the confines of the panels of the cupboard doors in this bathroom. The basic idea can very easily be applied to a variety of areas, whether it be on a folding screen, in a niche, or as shown here, in panels on a wall. Apart from being highly decorative, it allows one to put together a collection of china that would otherwise be out of one's reach, too rare or too expensive. There are, of course, situations where it would be unwise or inappropriate to have the real thing anyway, such as in a confined space where china could be easily knocked or damaged.

It helps when painting china to have the light from one direction, both to give form and to cast a shadow that aides the three dimensional effect.

Above: *One of a pair of Chelsea Red Anchor porcelain dishes that I used in the arrangement opposite. This factory had a relatively short life, producing the Red Anchor mark from 1752-58, but during that time it made some of the most enchanting and desirable soft-paste porcelain.*

PRACTICE

In 1968 the celebrated interior decorator John Fowler took me to Basildon Park in Berkshire to paint some grisaille panels in the drawing room for Lord and Lady Iliffe. There I met Jim Smart, who was responsible for the painted decoration of the room, and he introduced me to Flashe, an indelible gouache paint made by Lefranc at Bougeois. I found the paint sympathetic, and as a result used it for my largest commission, the south staircase at Ragley Hall, in Warwickshire, which I started a few months later. I have used these paints since that time and will always be grateful to Jim Smart for making me aware of them.

There are many books on paints, materials, and techniques available to those who wish to investigate further some of the alternative methods of wall painting, so I will not elaborate on these methods here.

Some painters have attended art school, some are self taught, while others may have worked in the studio of a practicing mural painter, or perhaps a little of all three. However, with the breakdown of the studio system, this is not an easy route to take. What is absolutely essential is to be able to draw, for without the knowledge of structure gained through drawing, it is difficult to simplify and abstract later on. I have always wanted to paint, with the result that apart from some help in the last decade, I have always worked alone. Had I built up a studio, it would have meant drumming up business and overseeing the work of others instead of painting myself.

Before starting out on a career as a mural painter it is worth spending some time to reflect on what it is that you wish to achieve. One of the most commonly asked questions is, "How do I start?" Difficult to answer, but one thing to try and hold on to is what inspires you, and what you would like to paint. If you imitate artists who are fashionable, you will never be as good as the person who really believes in what they are doing. Another important thing to bear in mind is that no one is going to divine that you are a genius if you remain undiscovered in your garret, so you must endeavour to show your work to as many people as possible. I was given some excellent advice in my middle twenties by Sir Jack Baer who gave me my first London exhibition at the Hazlitt Gallery: "Don't overprice your work, sell as much as possible, and you will gradually build up a following. This is how Henry Moore and Graham Sutherland started out." The same applies to mural painting. If you can paint a mural for someone at a reasonable price, hopefully it will lead to another! When you have too many commissions, you can put your prices up.

After discussing the subject matter with the client and having measured up, a design should be produced to scale, perhaps 1" or ½" to the foot, according to the size of the project. Having presented this, you may need to make alterations or even start again. However, it is important to do this in order that there is no surprise when the painting appears on the wall. For both you and your client, it is better to give a fixed price for the work. If you agree on an hourly or daily fee, you will forever have someone looking over your shoulder, which is not relaxing or conducive to making a good job of it.

As far as charging is concerned, I usually suggest that one third is payable on commencement of the work, one third half way through, and the remainder on completion. Expenses such as travel and hotel, etc, should be listed separately so that the client can decide if he or she would prefer to suggest a different arrangement—e.g., stay en famille, rather than in an hotel. Always try and clarify financial and other arrangements in advance as it saves upset later.

Yellow orche

Senegal yellow

Emerald oxide

Rose Tyrian

Ultramarine blue

Raw Sienna

Lemon yellow

Verdaccio

Ruby red

Cobalt blue

Burnt sienna

White

Cadmium red deep

Manganese blue

Raw umber

Black

Breughel red

Red orche

Above: My basic palette of colours. I have already mentioned that for the majority of my mural painting I use the water based, indelible gouache paints manufactured by Lefranc et Bourgeois under the trade name Flashe. The names of pigment above are from their list. I buy large jars of white pigment and small jars of the other colours as they tend to dry up if you don't use them.

WORKING METHOD

Before starting to paint a mural, the first step is to ensure that you have a good surface on which to work. Although you can paint directly onto the plaster wall, I find that this is the least sympathetic surface. I prefer a good quality rag paper, preferably with a scrim underneath so that it can be removed in the future if necessary. Canvas applied to the wall is another option, but it has more of a tooth.

Having made a design in watercolour, hopefully to scale, the next step is to square it up. To do this, cover the design with cellophane and working with a ball point pen divide it equally both vertically and horizontally to form a grid. In some instances you may use a larger grid overall, sub-dividing the more complicated areas. Then draw out the grid in charcoal onto the wall in exactly the same manner. You can then copy your design onto the wall using the reference points of the grid. When this is complete, lightly dust the charcoal and paint the design in line in red ochre or raw sienna, correcting the drawing as necessary. Finally, wipe off the grid and any surplus charcoal lines with a damp cloth.

Now that you have your design in line on the wall, the next step is to start blocking in the main areas of colour, lightly painting over the lines as you go so that they will show through. Having done this, in the case of a landscape, begin painting from the most distant point—i.e., the sky—and gradually work your way toward the foreground from the horizon. There will be a certain amount of to-ing and fro-ing, but this way you will be able to achieve the best relationship between colour, light, and shade. If the painting becomes too hard, light washes will help diffuse and soften the image. I prefer not to seal the finished work, although in some cases a flat varnish is necessary.

Above: *This photograph shows the design squared up, ready to use to copy onto the wall. If your design is in watercolour, you may find it easier to first trace a line drawing from it, to square up, as it is easier to see what is what.*

Cut a piece of cardboard to the same size as the drawing or watercolour to fit underneath, to make it firm to hold, and cover the drawing with cellophane taped at the back. You can then draw out your grid on the cellophane, using a ball point pen alternating solid and dashed lines to make it easier to read.

Right: Having noticed some rather healthy looking cabbages growing in the field of a Suffolk neighbour, I asked him if I might have one. He kindly dug one up and I quickly transported it to my studio and put it in a bucket of water. It was not the easiest of subjects to paint, as first it wilted, then revived, then relentlessly changed shape. When I had finished painting it, we ate it for dinner, with grated nutmeg, and it was delicious!

Above: *Wandering one afternoon in the shade of the trees at the foot of the Acropolis in Baalbek, I came upon a field which was blue with cabbages, and it seemed as if a thousand white butterflies were fluttering in the sun. I sat down with my sketch book under a mulberry tree laden with fruit and started to draw. I was joined later by a goatherd, who silently fed me white mulberries until he tired and retreated to his flock—et in arcadia ego!*

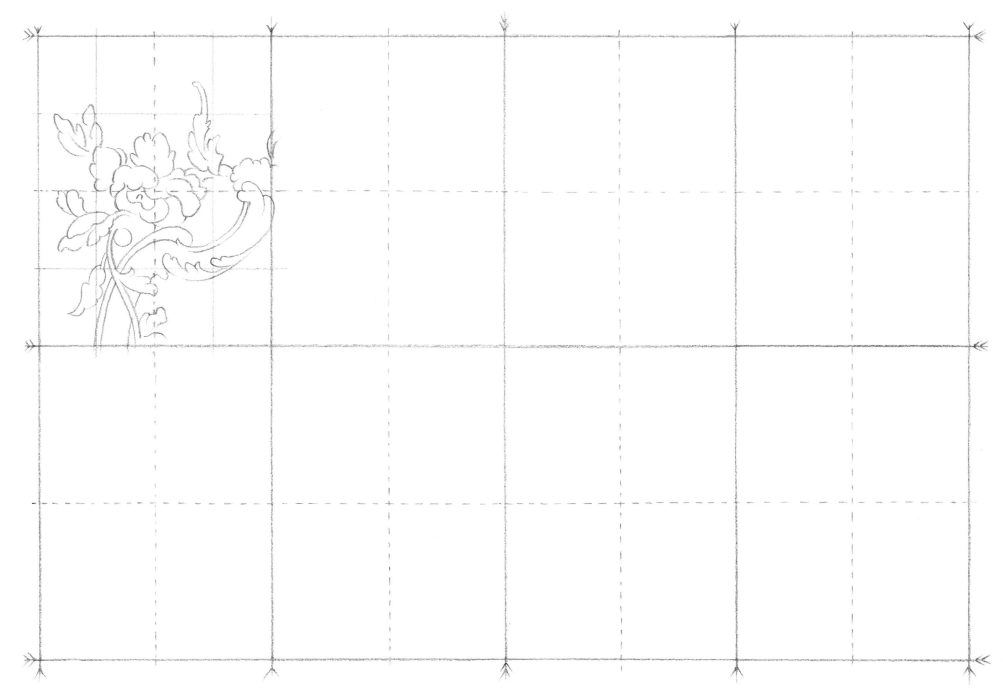

Above: *Having prepared your wall, the next stage is to draw out the grid that you have on you design, in charcoal, on the wall. When you have finished, dust it lightly so that it is still visible, and start drawing out the design, again in charcoal, using the reference points created by the grid. If you need more reference points, sub divide the relevant square or rectangle further on both the wall and the design.*

Above: *Here you have the whole drawing in charcoal plus the grid. Before the next stage it is advisable to dust off the charcoal lightly with a brush, so that when you come to paint over the lines you do not pick up too much black dust.*

Above: *The charcoal drawing of the design has now been painted in red ochre. Allow a little while for the paint to dry properly before trying to remove the residue of the drawing and grid. You can use a damp rag, but inevitably if you rub too hard at this stage you will take the paint off too.*

Above: *At this stage the blocking in of the colour takes place. You do not have to be too careful as you will need to work over it anyway. You will lose the red ochre lines, but they will reappear in a shadowy outline when the paint dries, and gradually be eliminated as you build up to a finish.*

Above: *The process from now on is one of building up the painting, having laid in the main areas of colour. The sky is the first to be finished, then slowly working from the far distance the landscape takes form. To a degree it needs to be worked together in order to get the colours and tones right. If you find it too strong, then washes of lighter colour will soften the effect.*

Above: *A delicate balance needs to be achieved as you finish the painting. Too much niggling can deaden the effect, so you have to judge when you think that it is time to stop. Elements such as the butterflies are easier to superimpose on the finished painting, as working around them, especially in plain areas, is inhibiting. Cast shadows from the plasterwork frame could be added to give it a sense of place, rather than appearing as a cutout.*

Acknowledgments

I would like to take the opportunity of thanking my editor, Paula Breslich, for her extreme patience with the endless stream of unmet deadlines. I am sure that she must have felt that getting work from me was like squeezing blood from a stone!

Also my gratitude to Lisa Tai for her clear, logical arrangement of my drawings in her elegant design for this book, and not least to Lucinda Macdonald who stepped into the breach at the eleventh hour to decipher my handwriting and type up my manuscript.

Finally a big thank you to all my friends and clients for allowing me to reproduce the drawings paintings and photographs included here. For the latter, my thanks go once again to Shona Wood.

The author and publisher would like to thank the following people for allowing work from their collections to be reproduced in this book.

Pages	
20-23	Mr & Mrs Richard Compton
24-27	Mr & Mrs John Rowe
28-31	Mr & Mrs Yehia Ghandour
50	The Viscountess Tamworth
53	Mrs Harald Mergard
53	Miss Claire Attenborough
54-57	Herr & Frau Dietmar Harting
66	Timothy Rootes Esq
66	The Hon. Mrs Christopher Sharples
77-73	Mr & Mrs Thomas Saunders III
92-97	Mr & Mrs Michael Abrahams
Cover	Mr & Mrs Michael Abrahams
133	Mrs Myrna Bustani
141	Miss Georgina Ellis
155	The Earl of Clanwilliam
156-157	Mr & Mrs Martyn Hedley
158	The Hon. Mrs Bonas
158	Mrs Harald Mergard
159	The Lady King of Wartnaby
159	Mrs Beverley Battersby
162-163	Mrs Tamara Malcolm
164-165	Prince Rupert Zu Loewenstein
164-165	The Fathers of the London Oratory
166	Mr & Mrs Charles Brocklebank
171	The Hon. Mrs Townshend
175	Timothy Scott-Bolton Esq